# A NEW RITE:

# CONSERVATIVE

# CATHOLIC

# ORGANIZATIONS

# AND THEIR ALLIES

Researched and Written by Steve Askin for Catholics for a Free Choice

This publication was made possible by a grant from the Robert Sterling Clark Foundation.

# ACKNOWLEDGEMENTS

A number of experienced journalists and researchers generously shared information and experience they have gathered through their own research on religious political action generally or the "Religious Right" more specifically. This would be a far less accurate and complete report were it not for the assistance of Russ Bellant, Chip Berlet, Rachel Burd, Carole J. L. Collins, Sara Diamond, and Craig Lasher.

Staff at the Catholic University Library (Washington), the Foundation Center (Washington), the National Charities Information Bureau (New York), the New York Secretary of State's Office of Charities Information (Albany), the Philanthropic Advisory Service of the Better Business Bureau (Arlington, VA), and Planned Parenthood Federation of America provided important advice on locating financial data and other information. Masimba Tafirenyika, Jane Hunter, and Denise Shannon and Chris Gould of Catholics for a Free Choice provided crucial research and editorial assistance.

Steve Askin

*Steve Askin is a writer with more than fifteen years' experience examining the fiscal and social performance of both non-profit and for-profit organizations. His investigative reporting has appeared in* Business Week, *the* Christian Science Monitor, *the* National Catholic Reporter, *and many other publications. He is a co-author of* Landmines: A Deadly Legacy *(New York: Human Rights Watch, 1993), and holds an MBA from the Columbia University School of Business.*

# TABLE OF CONTENTS

*Table of Contents, continued*

# INTRODUCTION

• • • • • • • • • • • • • • • • • • • • • • • • • • • • • • • • • • • • • •

## WHO'S RIGHT? CATHOLICS AND THE CULTURE WAR

*by Frances Kissling and Denise Shannon*

The Catholic community is nothing if not diverse. Its 2,000–year history is replete with warmongering and peace-making, charity and greed, licentiousness and asceticism, love and hate. Catholics are at times one with, even leaders of the dominant culture. In other instances, the Catholic church shines as a countercultural beacon against state injustice and oppression. The church's present is no different from its past. With some 60 million adherents in the United States, one–quarter of the population, Catholics cover the gamut of political and cultural belief.

Still, for many, Catholic activism evokes images of peace workers plowing fields in Nicaragua. And the Religious Right calls to mind fundamentalist and evangelical Protestants, not Roman Catholics. Yet there is a long tradition of Catholics participating in all levels of the work of the Religious Right, and the Catholic hierarchy has its own peculiar history with the movement.

It was a Catholic — the New Right strategist Paul Weyrich, founder of the Free Congress Foundation and the Heritage Foundation — who concocted the phrase "moral majority" and who designed the agenda of the organization that went by that name.[1] It was the willingness of the Catholic bishops to speak out "courageously" on abortion that Jerry Falwell cited as the stimulus for his own entry into the political sphere.[2] Phyllis Schlafly, anti–feminist crusader; William Bennett, roving moralist and possible future presidential candidate; Patrick Buchanan, Republican candidate for president in 1992 and purveyor of nativist, isolationist right–wing polemics — all are Catholics.

In inventing the Moral Majority for the Protestant Religious Right, Weyrich must have concluded that although Catholics inhabited the upper echelons of the Religious Right and the "New Right" wing of the conservative movement, there was not sufficient grassroots support or an alternative organizing strategy for a Catholic conservative movement. But times change.

### SOME BACKGROUND

The affinity between the Catholic right and the better–known Protestant Religious Right makes for a kind of ideological Möbius strip: the two distinct facets come together in a way that renders them indistinguishable. To understand the Catholic right, it helps to know the Protestant Religious Right.

Beginning in the 1970s, with religious orthodoxy as their banner, Religious Right supporters sought — and continue to seek — to create public policies that affirm their vision of private and public morality. The right wing of the Republican party became the political home of the Religious Right, and the first wave of the movement crested with the election to the presidency of soul mate Ronald Reagan. During Reagan's two terms, the right reveled as its values and aims began to be translated into public policy. The Bush years saw the Religious Right fade from public view, in part because such movements thrive in adverse climates, not victory, and partly because the East Coast establishment milieu of the Bush administration was less amenable to the Religious Right than were Reagan's heartland operatives. But behind the scenes, players sharpened political skills and honed ideological themes.

Now, the Religious Right has been reignited by the election of a Democratic president. With the rising prominence of organizations like the Christian Coalition, the Religious Right is again a significant feature on the political and cultural landscape. And Catholics remain a prominent part of the tableau. From the Old Right's William Buckley to the New Right's Weyrich, and from Buchanan to Bennett, these Catholic conservatives proclaim that their political convictions are based on their religious beliefs.

### THE CATHOLIC RIGHT

To the extent that they have been a political bloc in the United States, Catholics most often have been associated with progressive politics: labor struggles, the civil rights movement, and the Democratic party. US Catholics still tend to vote for Democrats (Catholics supported Clinton over Bush in the 1992 presidential election by 44 percent to 35 percent).[3] But a coterie of conservative Catholic leaders and thinkers coalesced during the 1980s in reaction to the liberal political activism of the American Catholic bishops on economic and military issues. They were in the right place at the right time: just as conservatives were searching for ways to reach out to new

*Introduction, continued*

constituencies, and just as a new pope began to make his leadership felt. Since his election in 1978, Pope John Paul II has named conservatives to positions of power in the church, applied considerable pressure to those with liberal views, and rewarded those clerics and lay Catholic leaders who see things his way.

"The most powerful fundamentalist of them all," journalist Penny Lernoux observed, "at least in terms of the number of followers he commands, is . . . Pope John Paul II."[4] Add the pope's anti–Communist crusade to his conservative family agenda, fierce opposition to abortion and contraception, lack of recognition of women's rights, an authoritarian style of leadership, and one sees a near perfect reflection of the agenda of the Religious Right. John Paul II, Jerry Falwell once declared, is "the best hope we Baptists ever had."[5]

### STRANGE BEDFELLOWS

As political strategists sifted through the moral issues in the early 1980s, one issue — abortion — stood out as capable of bridging differences among several constituencies — Protestant fundamentalists, the New Right, orthodox Catholics — and rallying a base of followers.[6] More than any other single issue, abortion came to define one's place on the political spectrum.

"It [abortion] is the symbol for a cultural cleavage between those with a sense of community and responsibility and the votaries of imperial individualism," said Weyrich, "between those whose sons fought in Vietnam and those whose sons chanted mantras for the victories of Ho Chi Minh; between those who worship in churches and those who desecrate them; between those who accept our culture and those who seek to tear it down."[7]

Thus, an odd alliance — seemingly oblivious to historical conflicts among the partners — was formed around the one issue of abortion. The Catholic bishops, once the whipping boys of conservatives for their pastorals advocating peace and a justice–based economy, began to count as their closest allies some of the most conservative, even reactionary, politicians and activists. A recent photo in the *National Catholic Reporter* recorded the strange union. Seated on a dais are cardinals John O'Connor, Bernard Law, Anthony Bevilacqua, James Hickey, and Roger Mahony, while pounding away at the podium before a "March for Life" audience is a stern–faced Jesse Helms, famed archconservative Republican senator from North Carolina.

"At present," writes political scientist Edward Sunshine, "no other public policy issue receives such uncompromising and relentless opposition from [Catholic] church leaders as does abortion."[8] So even though the bishops and Helms take opposing positions on virtually every social question except reproductive issues, they are political pals.

Still, the photograph oversimplifies. The bishops' political activism remains shot through with liberal strands. Whether the issue is health care, the economy, militarism, or civil rights, the bishops' positions reflect a tradition of generosity to the deprived, the vulnerable, and the marginalized. But this liberalism is starkly absent when it comes to abortion and the issues inextricably connected — women, the family, and sexuality. On these issues, church leaders do not apply the standard of justice that undergirds all other positions. On these issues, the bishops and conservatives stand on common, frozen ground. In their shared vision, the paterfamilias of the Roman era is central and presiding over the state, the family, the children, and most of all, women.

### THE CONSERVATIVE AGENDA

Some ten years ago, Catholic theologian and ethicist Daniel Maguire asserted that for conservatives, the term "family" is a catchall. "Using 'family' as the model for the state, and 'family' issues as models for New Right legislative action, the so–called family question covers a broad terrain. It supplies New Right tactics for majority tyranny. It includes the New Right platform for male and heterosexual dominance in society. It covers the issue of public control of private morality in the abortion dispute. And it encompasses the New Right's plans for the education of our children." To the right wing, Maguire wrote, the state is the family writ large. "However, the family they project for us is fascist, sexist, and racist. So too is their state."[9] Since Maguire wrote those words, the Catholic right has emerged publicly in support of this agenda.

In compiling this directory, we attempted to identify the Catholic organizations — and their close collaborators — whose agendas support this conservative blueprint for family and society. Despite the bishops' support for just economic and other policies, their promotion of the same social agenda made their inclusion inescapable.

The overlap of the Catholic right with the Protestant Religious Right is considerable. Many national committee members of the Catholic Campaign for America, for instance, are long–time associates of Pat Robertson. In addition, the Catholic organizations in this directory often cooperate with groups such as the Family Research Council, the Christian Coalition, Operation Rescue, Focus on the Family, and the Traditional Values Coalition.

In 1993, for instance, the archdiocese of New York joined forces with the Christian Coalition to elect school board candidates who supported prayer in the schools and restrictions on condom distribution and who opposed curriculum plans to encourage tolerance for lesbians and gays. More than 100,000 voters guides produced by Pat Robertson's Christian Coalition were distributed in Catholic parishes throughout New York City. In 1994, Christian Coalition postcards urging members of Congress to thwart health care reform were distributed in Catholic churches. These joint efforts create a powerful force. "We can bring together thousands of churches in concert," Robertson observed only one month before the voting record distribution. "I'm convinced on the political scene that if the evangelical churches, the Roman Catholic churches, the Orthodox Jewish people, all of us will work together, we can elect anybody to any office at any level."[10]

## Modus Operandi

The Catholic right mirrors the Religious Right not only in its goals, but also in its tactics and style. The Catholic Campaign for America mimics the Christian Coalition's grassroots approach, with the goal of training conservative Catholics "to serve in leadership capacities at the local level."[11] Church leaders have learned to enlist parishioners to further the hierarchy's political goals. Early in 1994, parishes across the country distributed 18 million postcards urging the Congress to defeat a health care plan in which reproductive health services would include abortion. And Catholic conservatives have begun to copy televangelists' strategy of reaching the masses through their own cable and broadcasting networks. The National Empowerment Television, operated by Weyrich's Free Congress Foundation, transmits its conservative message 24 hours daily.

In addition, Catholic conservatives have adopted the tone of Religious Right rhetoric. Erstwhile candidate Buchanan's speech at the 1992 Republican convention typified the viciousness and vindictiveness of movement oratory. The bombast epitomized the conservative side in the culture war.

Others had paved the way. "It may not be with bullets and it may not be with rockets and missiles, but it is a war nevertheless," Weyrich once declared. "It is a war of ideology, it's a war of ideas, and it's a war about our way of life. And it has to be fought with the same intensity, I think, and dedication as you would fight a shooting war."[12]

## Who's Who

"To set one's self up as a new right pressure group," conservative journalist Smith Hempstone observed, "all that's required is a grievance, no sense of humor, a secretary, a mailing list, a photocopier, some rented office premises and second hand furniture."[13] Some of the organizations we list in this directory may indeed have begun that way; one or two — the Alliance of Catholic Women, for instance — could still be so described. But others, most prominently the Knights of Columbus and the United States Catholic Conference/National Conference of Catholic Bishops, are large organizations with significant resources and considerable access to the powerful.

In assembling the data for this directory, we briefly reviewed one crucial aspect of the listed organizations' financial behavior: how they allocate the money they raise from donors and funding agencies. We did this by using the most widely recognized standards for charities' financial conduct, those promulgated by the non-partisan, New York-based National Charities Information Bureau (NCIB). NCIB's set of nine standards provide a yardstick for measuring performance in such areas as appropriateness of management structure, willingness to publicly disclose financial data, general fundraising integrity, meaningfulness of annual reports, financial accountability, and appropriate "use of funds."

Because a full NCIB-style review of an organization is complex and time-consuming, our analysis is limited to one standard — appropriateness of "use of funds" — on which full information can be found in a group's public tax return, the IRS Form 990. Under this standard, NCIB says that groups should devote no more than 40 percent of their annual spending to overhead and fundraising. The fact that some listed organizations satisfy this "use of funds" standard does not necessarily mean that they display financial and managerial integrity in other areas.

A word about the arrangement of listings: Some of the organizations are Catholic by definition. These we arranged in three sections of the directory, according to size and influence. The fourth section, Allies, profiles organizations whose public image is secular or ecumenical, but whose leadership, frequent collaborators, or guiding principles are orthodox Catholic. Finally, in an effort to answer questions that might naturally arise about Catholics for a Free Choice, we added an appendix containing an entry on CFFC, including the same kind of information presented in the other reports.

Taken together, the conservative Catholic organizations in this directory form an imposing force in public life, with enormous potential to affect politics, public policy, and the church. If Weyrich is correct, and this is war, we do well to know the enemy.

## Endnotes

1    Dionne, E.J. Jr., *Why Americans Hate Politics*, New York: Simon & Schuster, p. 230.
2    Dionne, p. 224.
3    Barone, Michael, and Ujifusa, Grant, *The Almanac of American Politics* 1994, Washington, DC: National Journal, p. xxvii.
4    *Lernoux*, Penny, "The papal spiderweb – II: a reverence for fundamentalism," *The Nation*, Apr. 17, 1989.
5    Neuhaus, Richard John, "The Right to Fight," *Commonweal*, Oct. 9, 1981, p. 557.
6    McKeegan, Michele, *Abortion Politics*, New York: The Free Press, 1992, p. 23.
7    Political Research Associates publication: "Traditional Values, Racism, & Christian Theocracy.
8    "The Primacy of Abortion in the Moral Rhetoric of U.S. Catholic Bishops," *The Annual of the Society of Christian Ethics*, 1990.
9    Maguire, Daniel C., *The New Subversives*, New York: Continuum, 1982.
10   Robertson quoted at the National Religious Broadcasters Association in 1993 in Conn, Joseph L., "Unholy Matrimony," *Church & State*, Apr., 1993.
11   Catholic Campaign for America 1993 fundraising letter.
12   Weyrich quoted by Richard Viguerie in Dionne, 1991, p. 229.
13   McKeegan, 1992, p. 24.

# PART I:
# THE U.S. CATHOLIC HIERARCHY

· · · · · · · · · · · · · · · · · · · · · · · · · · · · · · · · · · · · · · · · · · · · · · · · ·

## UNITED STATES CATHOLIC CONFERENCE / NATIONAL CONFERENCE OF CATHOLIC BISHOPS

*Committee (Secretariat) for Pro–Life Activities*
*3211 Fourth Street NE*
*Washington, DC 20017–1194*
*Tel: 202–541–3070*
*Fax: 202–541–3054*

### MEMBERSHIP, STRUCTURE, FINANCES

*Membership and structure[1]*

The **National Conference of Catholic Bishops (NCCB)** was organized to serve as an ecclesiastical body, linked to the Vatican, through which US bishops act together. The NCCB sponsors the **US Catholic Conference (USCC),** a civil corporation and 'secretariat' through which the NCCB and other church members act "for the good of society." The membership of both bodies consists of the more than 300 Catholic bishops — including both ordinaries (bishops who head dioceses) and auxiliary bishops — as well as cardinals serving in the United States, its territories and possessions. NCCB "Committees," composed of bishops, have associated operational "Secretariats," whose staff members carry out their day–to–day activities. While a distinct rationale exists for each entity, so far as social and political action is concerned there exists no significant functional difference between the NCCB and the USCC. For all practical purposes, both names refer to the same institution.

The USCC was created in 1967 (replacing the National Catholic Welfare Association) as the "operational secretariat and service agency of the NCCB for carrying out the civil–religious work of the church in this country." It effectively implements goals defined by the NCCB through its various committees, including the **Committee for Pro–Life Activities**.

The USCC/NCCB carries out its work through a national staff and through the efforts of a number of state–level Catholic conferences. State and national bodies have active lobbying programs on issues of concern to the USCC/NCCB. USCC/NCCB members serve on a variety of committees, among them the (Committee for Pro–Life Activities.) The Secretariat for Pro–life Activities coordinates prolife activities for the NCCB, in close collaboration with the USCC's Family Life Division.

*Financial data*

As church organizations, USCC, NCCB, the state conferences, the dioceses and most directly affiliated organizations are exempt from almost all federal and state financial disclosure requirements.[2] Their financial operations therefore cannot easily be compared with those of other non–profit organizations or assessed for compliance with non–profit sector financial standards. Nor is it possible to measure the full extent of prolife (or other) spending by the bishops and subordinate bodies.

However, the USCC/NCCB voluntarily makes public a substantial amount of budgetary data. Additional information is available from the published financial statements of the **Knights of Columbus**, which provides much of the funding for USCC/NCCB prolife activity.[3]

The USCC/NCCB budget totalled $43 million in 1993. It employs about 400 people, including 300 at the shared headquarters in Washington, DC. Key financial facts include the following:

- The prolife activities office is the best funded of the USCC/NCCB's 13 secretariats and committees, with a budget of $1.82 million in 1993 ($1.86 million is planned for 1994). This is more than three times the next largest budget, that of the Secretariat for Ecumenical and Interreligious Affairs, and four times the budget of the Secretariat for Laity, Women, Family, and Youth.
- The prolife activities office is only one — and probably not the largest — of several USCC/NCCB entities which spend money on prolife litigation, lobbying, organizing and outreach. While the exact amounts of money which they devote to prolife work are unknown, several units of USCC/NCCB provide shared services used by all the issue–specific committees and secretariats, including those

engaged in antichoice work. The 1993 budgets of key specialized service units which appear to contribute substantially to the antichoice effort were:

• Communications ($10.8 million);
• Legal counsel ($1.18 million); and
• Government liaison ($510,000).

About 75 percent of the prolife secretariat's budget comes from sources other than the bishops' General Fund, primarily the Knights of Columbus. Central funding is, however, only a small part of the story. Each diocese has its own diocesan budget and, in 28 states, bishops are organized into state Catholic conferences.

The USCC/NCCB also exercises ultimate authority over the abortion and family planning–related practices and policies of affiliated organizations, including Catholic Charities USA (domestic social programs) and Catholic Relief Services (international relief and development), both of which are controlled by the church but receive substantial government funding.

### PUBLICATIONS AND COMMUNICATION

The prolife secretariat's "Respect Life" program has an extensive catalog of manuals, flyers, brochures, church documents, films, videos and bumper stickers which are made available to dioceses, parishes and other abortion opponents. Most are produced for the secretariat by the USCC Office of Publishing and Promotional Services. Its regular publications include *Life Insight*, a monthly newsletter funded by the Knights of Columbus, and *Life At Risk*, a monthly newsletter on euthanasia funded at least through the end of 1993 by Our Sunday Visitor Foundation.

The USCC/NCCB has used several outside public relations firms with funds from the Knights of Columbus to advance its antichoice agenda:

• Its controversial $3 million to $5 million 1990 contract with Hill & Knowlton was cancelled in January 1992; the official explanation was that the prolife activities staff had been trained to perform the relevant tasks;[4]
• The Wirthlin Group has provided polling services; and
• As of November 1993, Capitoline International was their public relations firm (again funded by Knights of Columbus).

### POLICIES AND ACTIVITIES

*Historical overview: the shift to the right*

The USCC/NCCB takes positions on an enormous range of domestic and international questions. Its national legislative program for the 102nd Congress, 1991– 92, for instance, identified 74 "issues of concern to the bishops."[5]

Before abortion became a major public issue, the USCC/NCCB's domestic policy priorities — rooted in Catholic teachings on economic justice — made it a key and relatively consistent partner in domestic policy coalitions with liberal Democrats and organized labor.[6]

The USCC/NCCB was (and remains) hard to pigeonhole on international questions, primarily because the bishops are often genuinely divided. During the Cold War, fervent anti–communism took priority for some leading members of the hierarchy, while others pushed the conference to oppose human rights abuses perpetrated by pro–western dictatorships. Similarly, some bishops stressed the church's "just war" tradition, while others — arguing that the threat of nuclear holocaust made 'proportionate' use of military force all but impossible — moved toward a near pacifist position.[7] These divisions, of course, mirrored the splits within the Democratic Party, which (very broadly speaking) remained the political home of the preponderance of Catholic church leaders for at least the first three decades of the post World War II–era.

In the 1970s, the rise of the abortion issue pushed the bishops, for the first time in the modern era, onto political terrain where their allies were overwhelmingly Republican. Any drift toward broad coalition with conservative Republicans was slowed, however, by the election of President Ronald Reagan in 1980. Reagan's domestic economic agenda was anathema to most Catholic bishops. His administration's push for increased military spending and support for pro–western Third World dictatorships distressed many centrist bishops (though, as is documented by Lernoux and Hebblethwaite, it was greeted with favor by several leading cardinals and, ultimately, by Pope John Paul II himself). Nor were relations between church and president helped by the Reagan administration's aggressive use of its Catholic supporters to publicly confront the bishops.[8]

By contrast, President George Bush's approach to the bishops did much to foster the growth of links between the hierarchy and Republican leadership. Reversing the Reagan administration strategy, the Bush administration reached out to the hierarchy on issues on which they agreed, such as abortion, the family, parochial school aid and pornography. At the same time, Bush avoided public confrontations with the bishops on such divisive issues as domestic economic policy and international human rights.[9]

External conservative critics have largely failed to wean the USCC/NCCB from its generally liberal stands on domestic economic policy. They have had only limited impact on its approach to international and military questions. Citing the bishops' formal policy statements, conservatives often characterize the USCC/NCCB as a liberal–leaning organization.[10]

Yet an examination of bishops' actions in the political arena leads necessarily to a very different conclusion. In recent years, most, if not all, overt interventions in electoral politics by the USCC/NCCB's member bishops have involved coalitions with the Religious Right on abortion and other "family values" issues. The most vivid recent example — accurately described by *The New York Times* as a "tactical alliance" between the Roman Catholic Archdiocese of New York and Rev. Pat Robertson's Christian Coalition — involved the distribution in all Manhattan, Bronx and Staten Island Catholic parishes of a pamphlet designed to encourage voters to support school board candidates who favored prayer in the schools and restrictions on school–based distribution of condoms and opposed a sex education curriculum designed to encourage tolerance for homosexuals.[11] Though bishops almost never speak of their party affiliations, New York Auxiliary Bishop Austin Vaughan has said that Democratic support for prochoice positions motivated him to quit the Democratic party.[12]

On foreign policy questions, even where the USCC/NCCB issues "liberal" position statements, individual conservative bishops — men like Cardinal Bernard Law of Boston or Cardinal John O'Connor of New York— have often taken a far more activist stance which not infrequently lined them up with the Republican right. (See, for example, separate listing on the **Knights of Malta**.)

*On sexuality and reproductive issues*

The USCC/NCCB, like the Holy See, opposes legal abortion under all circumstances, supports natural family planning, and opposes artificial contraception.  In recent years, the USCC/NCCB has added to its antichoice agenda highly publicized diocesan efforts to assist poor and low income women who want to carry their pregnancies to term. No financial data are available on these efforts, but sporadic reviews suggest they are largely focused on securing govern-ment assistance for these women and scoring political points rather than using church resources.

The USCC/NCCB, which has long played a leading role in US antichoice activities, helped launch the modern antichoice movement in the aftermath of the Supreme Court decision *Roe v. Wade* (1973). The USCC's Family Life Division provided the initial support for creation of the National Right–to–Life Committee, though it cut direct ties with NRLC soon thereafter, at least partly to insulate itself against challenges to its tax exempt status. In March 1974 — in the first congressional hearing appearance by any Catholic cardinal — cardinals John Krol of Philadelphia, Humberto Madeiros of Boston, John Cody of Chicago and Timothy Manning of Los Angeles jointly testified in support of a Human Life Amendment before the Senate Judiciary Committee.[13] In 1975, the bishops issued their "pastoral program for prolife activities" which called for establishment of prolife action groups in every congressional district, support for election of antichoice candidates to local political posi-tions, and establishing files on the positions on legal abortion of all official and potential candidates for political office.

At their 1989 annual meeting, the bishops called abortion the number one human rights issue and called on Catholics to "commit themselves vigorously" to the goal of criminalizing abortion. Starting soon after that vote, the bishops increas-ingly used religious sanctions as a way of achieving political ends. For example, in 1989, San Diego's Leo T. Maher, now deceased, informed California state senate candidate Lucy

Killea, a prochoice Catholic, that she could no longer receive communion because of her position on abortion. In 1990, several bishops, including bishops John C. Reiss of Trenton, New Jersey, James T. McHugh of Camden, New Jersey, and New York's Cardinal John O'Connor barred prochoice Catholic officeholders and candidates from speaking at church–sponsored events in their dioceses. Peoria Bishop John J. Myers wrote that it is "immoral for church members to vote for candidates who favor abortion rights."[14]

Still, tensions have long existed between the USCC/NCCB and some of the more militant antichoice groups on tactics and political goals. Levels of militancy also vary among the member bishops. Until 1988, when Auxiliary Bishop Austin Vaughan of New York was arrested at an Operation Rescue protest, bishops uniformly avoided open displays of support for clinic blockades and other militant action. Following Vaughan's example, bishops George E. Lynch of North Carolina (retired), Paul V. Dudley (Sioux Falls, South Dakota) and Albert H. Ottenweller (Steubenville, Ohio) were soon arrested at similar protests.[15] While not participating personally, New York's Cardinal John O'Connor first endorsed the clinic blockade tactic in 1989, the year he became head of the bishops' prolife activities committee. Three years later, O'Connor participated in a "prayer vigil" outside a Manhattan clinic. Los Angeles Cardinal Roger Mahony, who succeeded O'Connor as head of the prolife committee in 1993, has also endorsed clinic blockades.[16]

After the killing of a doctor who provided abortions in March 1993, many observers singled out for praise the statement issued on behalf of the USCC/NCCB by their spokeswoman Helen Alvaré: "As we abhor the violence of abortion, we abhor violence as a dangerous and deplorable means to stop abortion," the second sentence in the four–sentence statement read. Given how offensive many anti-choice reactions were, the bishops' statement seemed more moderate. However, even the bishops compared the violence of Dr. Gunn's murder with the "violence of abortion," contin-uing to use the very comparison that provides unbalanced individuals with justification for their violent acts.[17]

NCCB members have remained publicly divided in their attitude toward prochoice Catholic politicians. While many bishops have insisted that prochoice politicians should be sanctioned and some support excommunication, others, including Cardinal Joseph Bernardin of Chicago, have opposed such action.[18]

That tactical divisions persist can be seen in remarks from Vaughan, who remains the bishop most active in the Rescue movement. At the June 1992 NCCB meeting he led the opposition to a proposed pastoral letter on women, complain-ing that it failed to address the "problem" of feminism and spoke "apologetically" on abortion and contraception.[19] In 1993, Vaughan joined lay members of "Citizens for Life" in a statement which, while arguing that it was unwise for prolifers to kill doctors, insisted that "those who take up arms against abortionists cannot be simply condemned, nor are they guilty

*United States Catholic Conference / National Conference of Catholic Bishops, continued*

of murder."[20]

In November 1993, the NCCB voted unanimously to ask the prolife committee to draft a "new, fresh, compelling" pastoral letter on abortion, the first since 1975. The new letter is timed to coincide with an anticipated papal encyclical on human life, which is expected to address abortion and other issues.[21]

The USCC/NCCB rarely publicizes its stand on contraception, perhaps because of the overwhelming acceptance of contraception among Catholics. However, the USCC/NCCB does not support coverage of contraception in a national health care plan, and actively opposes government funding of contraceptive research, the distribution of contraception and information on birth control at school–based clinics, and the dissemination of condoms even in prevention programs for AIDS and other sexually transmitted diseases.

## PEOPLE
### Chair
Mahony, Cardinal Roger of Los Angeles

### Past Chairs
Law, Cardinal Bernard of Boston
O'Connor, Cardinal John of New York

### Secretariat staff include
Quinn, Gail P., Executive Director
Alvaré, Helen, Director, Information and Planning
Doerflinger, Richard, Associate Director, Policy Development

## ENDNOTES
1   The description of USCC/NCCB structure is drawn from the *Catholic Almanac*, the *Official Catholic Directory* and various USCC/NCCB publications.
2   United States Internal Revenue Service, *Cumulative List of Organizations described in section 170(C) of the Internal Revenue of 1986*, Revised to September 30, 1992, Preface, Part II. Also note that the NCIB does not attempt to assess compliance by churches with industry standards.
3   Unless otherwise noted, financial data presented here are taken from the NCCB/USCC *Agenda Report*

*Documentation for General Meeting, November 15–18, 1993* and the Knights of Columbus financial data contained in the October 1993 issue of *Columbia*.
4   *New York Times*, May 13, 1990; *National Catholic Reporter*, Feb. 14, 1992.
5   CFFC 1991, p. 3.
6   To get a picture of this coalition in action, one might review the career of Msgr. George G. Higgins (See Costello 1984 and Higgins and Bole 1992), a long–time USCC official who personified the coalition for more than forty years.
7   For a conservative perspective on these complex currents, see Benestad 1980, or Weigel, 1989; for a liberal interpretation, see Lernoux, 1989 or Hebblethwaite, 1986.
8   Lernoux, 1987, esp. pp. 172–192. See also Hebblethwaite, 1986.
9   For a enlightening look at Bush's campaign to win favor among the bishops, see Feuerherd 1989; See also account of a Bush address to the Knights of Columbus in *The Wanderer*, Sept. 10, 1992.
10  See for example, Neuhaus 1993.
11  *New York Times*, Apr. 16, 1993; *Church & State*, June 1993.
12  *Milwaukee Journal*, Aug. 22, 1989.
13  Tribe, pp. 145–147.
14  *Guide for Prochoice Catholics: The Church, the State, and Abortion Politics*, CFFC, 1990, pp. 30 –36.
15  *Milwaukee Journal*, Aug. 22, 1989; Green Bay (WI) *News–Chronicle*, Oct. 2, 1989;
16  See *Milwaukee Journal*, Aug 22, 1989; *Los Angeles Herald–Examiner*, Aug. 12, 1989; *New York Times*, Oct. 2, 1989; *Los Angeles Times*, Oct. 21, 1989; *The Wanderer*, Dec. 10, 1992.
17  *Origins*, Mar. 25, 1993, p. 703.
18  See *New York Times*, May 13, 1990 and CFFC 1991.
19  *National Catholic Register*, July 5, 1992.
20  Citizens for Life, 1993.
21  *Washington Post*, Nov. 16, 1993.

# PART II:
# PROMINENT CATHOLIC ORGANIZATIONS

· · · · · · · · · · · · · · · · · · · · · · · · · · · · · · · · · · · · · · · · · · · · · · · · ·

## CATHOLIC CAMPAIGN FOR AMERICA

*1620 I Street NW, #716,*
*Washington, DC*
*Tel: 202–833–5569*

### MEMBERSHIP, STRUCTURE, FINANCES
#### Membership

At its founding in 1991, the **Catholic Campaign for America (CCA)** brought together conservative Catholic leaders, and was not a mass membership organization. As of October 1993, however, direct mail being distributed by CCA announced that the organization intended to use direct mail to contact 250,000 "potential new members" — who were asked to contribute $25 or more — within six months.[1]

#### Financial data[2]

Registered as a 501(c)(3) public charity.

Reported revenue of $244 thousand and expenditures of $159 thousand in 1992, its first full year of operations. Functional division of 1992 expenditures was as follows:

- Management and general expense: 58%
- Fundraising (professional fundraising fees): 42%
- Program services: 0%

CCA is the only group whose finances have been examined for this guide which allocated no funds for program activity and instead devoted all reported spending to overhead and fundraising. This represents a serious deviation from the voluntary standards established by the independent National Charities Information Bureau, the leading monitoring group for non–profit sector finance. NCIB recommends that organizations "spend at least 60% of annual expenses for program activities."[3] Given that 1992 was CCA's first full year of operation, one may need to review its 1993 financial documents before assessing the significance of this questionable spending pattern.

As of November 1993, CCA had not submitted the public disclosure documents required by the state of New York prior to direct mail or other fundraising efforts which aim to raise more than $25,000 from residents of that state. Unless New York residents were systematically excluded from the fall 1993 direct mail campaign, it would appear that CCA probably violated state law.[4]

### PUBLICATIONS AND COMMUNICATION
*Campaign Update,* quarterly newsletter.

### POLICIES AND ACTIVITIES[5]
#### Activities

CCA in theory: non–partisan Catholic action — Though CCA was founded in September 1991 by long–time religious right activist and Republican campaign official Marlene Elwell, it has consistently attempted to portray itself as a "non–partisan organization of concerned Catholic Americans." It has made efforts — such as sponsorship of a dinner honoring Pennsylvania Governor Robert Casey[6] and the inclusion of former New York Governor Hugh Carey on its board of directors — to show its support for anti–abortion Catholic Democrats. At the group's founding press conference, board member William Bennett insisted that "this is not a 'Republican Catholic Campaign for America' or a 'Conservative Catholic Campaign for America," and stressed his desire to recruit "Democrats and liberal Democrats."[7]

CCA in practice: a central committee for Catholic Republicanism — In practice, CCA's leadership is a "Who's Who" of Catholic Republicanism. Its leadership bodies include the two Republican presidential aspirants who most vociferously draw connections between their Catholic upbringing and current politics (William Bennett and Patrick Buchanan); two conservative Republican Members of Congress (Robert K. Dornan of California and Richard Santorum of Pennsylvania); former Treasury Secretary William Simon; former Senator Jeremiah Denton (Republican, Alabama); two Reagan–era ambassadors to the Vatican (Frank Shakespeare and William A. Wilson); and a host of other prominent Republicans. Ideologically, CCA's advisory body, the National Committee, bridges the political divisions within the Catholic right, bringing neoconservatives

*Catholic Campaign for America, continued*

like Fr. Richard J. Neuhaus of the **Institute on Religion and Public Life** together with leaders of such organizations as **Opus Dei** and the anti–democratic **Society for Tradition, Family and Property**.

Structurally, CCA seems to be closely related to Domino's Pizza magnate Thomas S. Monaghan's network of organizations and associates. CCA founder Elwell and executive director Wykes both served as officials of **Legatus** — Monaghan's club for Catholic corporate executives — before joining CCA. Legatus Michigan chapter chair Frank Stella serves on the National Committee.[8] National Committee members also include Rev. Michael Scanlan and Keith Fournier, who held top leadership positions in the Monaghan–backed **Word of God–Sword of the Spirit** network. A number of CCA backers — including Directors Thomas G. Ferguson and Robert Van Dine — are, like Monaghan, members of the **Knights of Malta**.

Carey — CCA's sole prominent Democrat — is an exception whose recent personal history proves the rule. The ex–governor–turned–businessman moved to the right after retiring from politics. Carey, who now works for J. Peter Grace — the pivotal figure in the 1980s alliance between conservative Catholicism and the Reaganite right — views CCA as the vehicle for moving Catholics "from a defensive to an activist position" as "members of the church militant."[9]

CCA's actions and public statements mark it as a would–be conservative Catholic faction within the Republican Party and as the closest Catholic equivalent to Pat Robertson's Christian Coalition. Indeed, several long–time Robertson operatives serve in the leadership of CCA. National Committee member Fournier is a charismatic Catholic who heads the American Center for Law and Justice (ACLJ), based at Pat Robertson's Regent University in Virginia Beach, Virginia. ACLJ enjoys close ties to **Catholics United for Life**. CCA co–founder Elwell worked for Robertson from 1985, when she joined the staff of his Freedom Council, through 1988, when she headed his midwestern presidential campaign organization. Elwell has argued that "in a lot of areas, the liberal Catholics' thinking is Communist–infiltrated."[10]

In a global Catholic context, CCA's orientation most closely resembles that of Catholic movements (such as Italy's Communion and Liberation) that have functioned as right–wing Catholic factions inside center–right European or Latin American political parties. Not content with opposition to abortion or "protection" of the freedom of Catholics to practice their religion, CCA aspires across a wide range of issues to state imposition of its set of Catholic cultural values. On the spectrum of US Catholic activism, CCA views itself (according to executive director Wykes) as the "pro–active" complement to the **Catholic League's** largely "defensive" activity.

CCA works actively and almost single–mindedly to promote Republican personalities, their political goals and their election to public office. The most visible public action

of CCA's first two years was the broadcast of TV commercials, under the theme "Vote Your Values," on the eve of the 1992 general election. Broadcast in Boston, Chicago, New York and Philadelphia, these ads stopped just short of Republican partisanship. Without naming candidates, they urged voters to vote for those who support school vouchers, legal protection for the unborn and a "wholesome moral environment." Would–be presidential candidate Bennett, who serves on the group's ten–member board of directors, has played a particularly prominent role in almost all of CCA's public events.[11]

Public statements stress a broad campaign of "grassroots" organizing, with a goal of establishing a base in at least 10 metropolitan areas by the end of 1994. Stated organizing objectives include:

- Recruiting "the greatest coalition of Catholic leaders in American history" by mobilizing them "at the national, state and local levels;"
- Increasing "the Catholic electorate's influence in formulating public policy and focus the public's attention on the richness and beauty of Catholic teaching;"
- Training Catholic citizens "to serve in leadership capacities at the local level;" and
- Creating "opportunities for Catholics to demonstrate to policy makers the power of an organized Catholic constituency."

However, it appears that only limited steps have been taken — in Michigan, Florida and perhaps one or two other states — to implement this program. Despite the rhetoric of grassroots organizing, it appears that CCA's main public events to date have been press conferences and "gala" dinners.

At the national level, CCA has made some efforts to collaborate with — and heighten the Catholic profile of — established groups rooted in the Protestant Religious Right. One such initiative involved an August 1993 press conference on Media Coverage of the Papal Visit. This event was co–sponsored with the Christian Coalition and featured a report by L. Brent Bozell, a Catholic who heads the Conservative Victory Committee and has long experience working with Protestant fundamentalists in right–wing coalition groups. Bozell charged that US news media, and especially the major TV networks, treated the papal visit as "an occasion to portray the Catholic church as out of touch with its hip American followers, while trumpeting polls decrying the church's supposed 'theological rigidity.'"[12]

### Policies

Policy statements are carefully framed in moderate language which conforms to the tone of recent encyclicals and professes faithfulness to the teachings of Vatican II. Yet right–wing politics — not loyalty to the pope and the magisterium — is the sole common denominator of CCA leadership. CCA's openness to even the anti–papal extreme right can be seen, for example, in the inclusion on its national committee of the US executive director of Tradition, Family and Property. CCA pronouncements say relatively little about Catholic social teachings on economic justice and international peace, while stressing cultural and "family" concerns which conform to the goals of recent Republican platforms. The few seeming exceptions (such as support for a "family wage") involve social services designed to encourage women to stay out of the workforce. On some issues, CCA seeks to protect the orthodox Catholic conscience from imposition of non–Catholic values (in sex education, for example); on others (such as abortion, contraception and surrogate motherhood), it demands imposition of an orthodox Catholic view of "objective moral law" upon non–Catholics.

*On sexuality and reproductive issues*

**Abortion:** An "unspeakable crime." Any law which permits abortion "is in itself immoral."

**Contraception:** "The objective moral order ... excludes recourse to contraception, sterilization and abortion... In international relations, economic aid for the advancement of peoples must not be conditioned on acceptance of programs of contraception, sterilization and abortion."

**The family:** "The family is the first and vital cell of society and exists prior to the state. The state exists to protect the religious, political, social and economic rights of the family."

**Homosexuality:** "Sexual relations between persons of the same sex are necessarily and inherently disordered according to the objective moral order. Homosexual acts are intrinsically disordered and may never be approved in any way whatsoever [but] persons afflicted with homosexual tendencies should not, on that account, be denied any rights of the person or of the citizen."

**Sex education:** "Parents have the right to ensure that their children are not compelled to attend classes which are not in agreement with their own moral and religious convictions."

**Surrogate motherhood:** "Civil law cannot legitimize the donation of gametes between persons who are not legitimately united in marriage. Legislation must prohibit, by virtue of the support which is due to the family, embryo banks, post mortem insemination, and 'surrogate motherhood'."

**Women:** "True advancement of women requires ... that recognition be given to their maternal and family roles in comparison to all other public roles and all other professions.... Remuneration for work must be sufficient for establishing and maintaining a family with dignity, either through a suitable salary, called a 'family wage', or through other social measures such as family allowances or the remuneration in the house of one of the parents; it should be such that mothers will not be obliged to work outside the home to the detriment of family life."

*Other issues*

**The economy:** "Every individual has the right to economic initiative and a right to private property while respecting the social and public character of ownership."

**Euthanasia:** "No one is permitted to ask for this act of killing, either for himself or herself or for another person entrusted in his or her own care, nor can he or she consent to it, either explicitly or implicitly. Nor can any authority legitimately recommend or permit such an action."

**Free expression:** "Everything in...social communication which arouses men's baser passions and encourages low moral standards, likewise every obscenity in the written word and every form of indecency on the stage and screen, should be condemned publicly and unanimously" and must not be protected by "the liberty which may be allowed in this field by public authorities."

**Parochial schools:** Asserts that compulsory education "from which all religious formation is excluded" violates "parents' freedom". Demands full and equal funding for parent–selected schools which provide "religious formation."

**State promotion of religion:** Argues that the government should "take account of the religious life of its citizenry and show it favor… and create conditions favorable to the fostering of religious life," though without "command[ing] or inhibit[ing] acts that are religious."

**War and peace:** War is "always an evil, at least in the natural order, although it may sometimes be morally necessary. In any case, the doctrine of a just war must be strictly observed."

## PEOPLE

*Leadership*

Elwell, Marlene, founder (long–time Republican activist; former Pat Robertson and George Bush campaign official; former director of Thomas S. Monaghan's Legatus)[13]

Wykes, Thomas V. Jr., Executive Director (Wykes was the only paid official in 1992)

O'Connor, Cardinal John of NY, National Ecclesiastical Advisor

*Board of directors*

Lynch, Frank J., Chairman of the Board

Allen, Richard V., first Reagan Administration National Security Advisor

Bennett, William J., Republican presidential hopeful; former Reagan and Bush administration official

Bork, Mary Ellen, Secretary, The John Carroll Society

Carey, Hugh L., Executive Vice President, W.R. Grace and Co, former New York Governor

Van Dine, Robert, Vice Chairman, St. Ives Laboratories Corp.

Ferguson, Thomas G., Chairman and CEO, Ferguson Communications Group

Gracida, Bishop Rene H., Bishop of Corpus Christi

Sasso, William R., Senior Partner, Stradley, Ronon, Stevens and Young

Shakespeare, Frank, former Vatican Ambassador, Former Director, US Information Agency

## *Catholic Campaign for America, continued*

***National Committee*[14] (*Affiliations as listed in CCA publication*)**

Aguirre, Dr. Horatio, Publisher, *Diario Las Americas*

Astarita, Joseph J., of Opus Dei, Vice President, Crawford Foundation.

Ball, William, Senior Managing Partner, Ball, Skelly, Murren & Connell

Bavaro, Mark, Philadelphia Eagles football team

Becker, Dee, March for Life

Best, Robert A., President, Private Sector Initiative

Brennan, John V., Chairman/CEO, US Aviation Underwriters, Inc.

Brown, Judie A., President, **American Life League**

Buchanan, Patrick J., Syndicated columnist

Carroll, Warren H., Chair, History Department, Christendom College

Clarke, Thomas R., Past State Deputy, Michigan **Knights of Columbus**

Collins, John F., Former Mayor, Boston

Coniker, Jerome, President, Apostolate for Family Consecration

Denton, Jeremiah A., former Alabama Senator

Dornan, Rep. Robert K. (R–California)

Fedoryka, Dr. Damien P., former President, Christendom College

Fessio, Rev. Joseph D. SJ, Publisher, *Catholic World Report*; founder/editor, Ignatius Press

Fournier, Keith, Executive Director, American Center for Law and Justice

Fox, Anne, Massachusetts Citizens for Life

Gail, Brian J., President, FCB Philadelphia

Godfrey, Christopher J., President, Pro–Life Athletes, Inc.

Goodwin, Karen, President, Fifth Avenue Productions

Gray, Nellie, President, March for Life

Grier, Dr. Delores Bernadette, Vice Chancellor, Archdiocese of New York

Haas, Dr. John M., Chair, Moral Theology, St. Charles Borromeo Seminary

Hahn, Scott, Associate Dean of Theology, **University of Steubenville**

Hanretty, Patrick M., FBI

Hartigan, Jack, Esq., author, lecturer

Healy, Michael J. Jr., Vice President University Relations, University of Steubenville

Henkels, Paul M. & Barbara, Chairman/CEO, Henkels & McCoy

Herron, Msgr. Thomas J., Academic Dean/Theology, St. Charles Borromeo Seminary

Hilbert, Donald, Major–Gen., USA Ret.; Director, US Soldiers & Airmen's Home

Hilgers, Thomas W., MD, Director, Pope Paul VI Institute

Hunt, Mary Reilly, Director of Development, National Right to Life Committee

Karcher, Carl N., Chairman/CEO, Carl Karchner Enterprises

Kelly, Molly, author/lecturer

King, Edward, former Massachusetts Governor

Kippley, John F., President, Couple to Couple League

Kuhn, Bowie, former Commissioner, Major League Baseball; President, The Kent Group

Kuprys, Saulius K., Pres., Lithuanian Roman Catholic Federation

Lauer, Paul, President, Veritas Communications

Lengyel, Dr. Alfonz, Exec V–P, National Federation of Hungarian Americans

Likoudis, James, Catholics United for the Faith

Lundy, Marilyn F., President, League of Catholic Women – Detroit

Maher, Joseph, Vice–President, Veritas Communications

Martino, Dr. Rocco L., Chairman/CEO, XRT

Matt, Alphonse J. Jr., Publisher/editor, *The Wanderer*

McCabe, James J. & Rose Marie, Chair, Litigation Department, Duane Morris & Heckscher

McInerney, Ralph, Publisher, *Crisis* magazine

Monaghan, Thomas Patrick, Catholics United for Life

Monaghan, Thomas S., CEO, Domino's Pizza

Molineaux, Charles B., Partner, Bastianelli, Brown & Touhey

Murray, James J., President, James Murray Ltd.

Neuhaus, Rev. Dr. Richard J.

Orsini, Dr. Jean Francois, TOP, President, St. Antoninus Institute

Palsbys, Audrone, Lithuanian Roman Catholic Federation of America

Petrini, Rev. Aldo P., Pastor, St. Mary's Catholic Church, Washington, DC

Petrusic, Rev. Anthony A., President, Croatian Catholic Union/USA

Piedra, Dr. Alberto, Catholic University of America

Reuter, Ted, President/CEO, Reuter Brewing Co.

Ring, John, **Catholic League for Religious and Civil Rights**

Roeser, Thomas F., President, Thomas F. Roeser & Associates

Ryan, Judge James L., United States Court of Appeals, Sixth Circuit

Santorum, Rep. Richard J., (R–Pennsylvania)

Scanlan, Rev. Michael TOR, President, Franciscan University of Steubenville

Schlafly, Phyllis, Eagle Forum; Republican National Coalition for Life

Schmieder, Steven, Executive Director, Tradition Family and Property

Shaw, Russell, Director, Office of Public Information, Knights of Columbus

Simon, William E., Chairman, William E. Simon & Sons, Inc. (former Secretary of the Treasury)

Speier, Chris, former San Francisco Giant baseball team

Stella, Frank G., Chair, Michigan Chapter Legatus and CEO F. D. Stella Products

Stravinskas, Rev. Peter, Editor, *Catholic Answer*

Tracy, Thomas J., President, Genuine Parts Distributors

Urbik, Jerome A., board member Republican National Coalition for Life and CEO Hinsdale Associates

Vaughan, Austin B., Auxiliary Bishop of New York

Wagner, David M., Director, Legal Policy, Family Research Council

Weaver, Joe, Editorial Director, WJBK – TV 2, CBS Affiliate, Detroit

Willke, Dr. Jack, MD, President, Life Issues Institute

Wilson, Kaye Lani Rae Rafko, Miss America 1988

Wilson, Mercedes Arzu, President, Families of the Americas Foundation

Wilson, William A., Former Ambassador to the Vatican

Winn, Michael, President/CEO, Holister Inc.

Woolsey, Rev. Msgr John G., Director, Respect Life office, New York Archdiocese

# HUMAN LIFE INTERNATIONAL

*7845 Airpark Road, Suite E*
*Gaithersburg, MD 20879*
*Tel: 301–670–7884*
*Fax: 301–869–7363*

*Miami office: Vida Humana Internacional*
*4345 SW 72nd Avenue, Suite E*
*Miami, FLA 33155*
*Tel: 305–662–1497*
*FAX: 305–662–1499*

*HLI in Canada, Inc.*
*191 Granville Street, Vanier, ON K1L 6Y3,*
*CANADA*
*Tel: (613)–745–9405*
*FAX: (613)–745–9868*

## MEMBERSHIP, STRUCTURE, FINANCES

### Structure

Though **Human Life International (HLI)** calls itself "the world's largest pro–life organization"[15] and an HLI spokesman recently claimed that HLI has 30,000 members,[16] neither of these claims is accurate.

HLI's tax returns show that the group has no dues paying membership, nor is it the "world's largest" as measured by annual revenue: a number of other anti–abortion groups — including the **American Life League**, have larger budgets.

HLI does, however, appear to maintain the US prolife movement's largest network of international affiliates.

### Chapters and branches[17]

In North America, HLI has 25 "quasi–independent" chapters and aims to establish at least one in each state and Canadian province in 1994. (States and provinces with an HLI chapter include California; Florida; Georgia; Hawaii; Illinois; Iowa; Louisiana; Maine; Massachusetts; Michigan; Missouri; New York; North Dakota; Ohio; Pennsylvania; Washington; and Alberta, Canada.) These chapters are designed as fundraising and literature sales auxiliaries to the central organization and receive no funding from HLI headquarters.

Internationally, HLI reports the existence of 53 branches in 39 countries. In practice, however, this branch network appears to consist of independent entities which receive donations and/or technical assistance from HLI. In some, and possibly most cases, the branches appear to be groups which were established independently by local Catholic church leaders or antichoice activists, which only later obtained grants from HLI.

HLI reports the existence of branches in:
North/Central America: Costa Rica; Mexico; Puerto Rico; Trinidad.
South America: Argentina; Brazil (2); Chile; Columbia (2); Ecuador; El Salvador; Paraguay; Peru; Uruguay.
Europe: Austria; Belgium; Croatia; Czech Republic; Germany; Netherlands; Hungary; Ireland (3); Poland (2); Slovak Republic; Slovenia; Sweden; Switzerland; UK (2); Ukraine (2).
Africa: Kenya; Lesotho; Nigeria; South Africa (2); Zimbabwe.
Asia: Australia; Burma; India (3); Malaysia (2); Philippines (2); Singapore; Sri Lanka.

HLI's Miami office, responsible for Latin America, distributes materials throughout the Portuguese and Spanish–speaking world.

### Other divisions and affiliates

• **HLI Endowment Inc.** (which donates materials, equipment and money to "non–profit" groups around the world and in the United States). Spending for this activity grew from $96,000 in 1990 to $1.8 million in 1992.

• **Population Research Institute** (PRI), Describes itself as "a non–profit, non–partisan group that carries out research on population, development and environmental issues."[18] Emphasis on attacking groups which support family planning, ranging from UNICEF to Planned Parenthood, and "proving" that over–population is not a problem for developing nations.

• **Pro–life/Family Institute**, "devoted to training and enabling pro–life leaders who will carry on Fr. Marx's work as future 'Apostles of Life'".

• **Humanae Vitae Priests, Religious and Laity International** (founded 1991).

HLI has also established the **World Council for Life and Family** (WCLF) "to create a unified worldwide network of pro–life/pro–family organizations and individuals."

HLI also "assists the activities" of **Seminarians for Life International**, "which is involved in the formation of pro–life priests."

As of 1993 HLI was forming a group for activist anti-choice nuns.

### Financial data[19]

Registered as a 501(c)(3) public charity.

Rapid expenditure growth (from $1.9 million in 1990 to $4.7 million in 1992) has not been matched by revenue growth ($2.7 million in 1990 to $3.8 million in 1992). The group nonetheless remains solvent based on surpluses built up in past years. Receipts and expenditures appear to cover domestic operations plus donations from the US organization to foreign "branches," but not local receipts and expenditures of those "branches."

HLI's reported functional breakdown of expenditures satisfies NCIB guidelines calling for application of at least 60 percent of funds to program services:

| | |
|---|---|
| • Management and general expense: | 6% |
| • Fundraising: | 8% |
| • Program services: | 86% |

Direct mail is its sole source of public contributions, which rose from $956,000 (1990) to $2.37 million (1992).

In addition to their salaries, at least two HLI officers have received below–market mortgages (in one case involving a property purchased from the organization) in recent years. Though these non–monetary fringe benefits are noted in HLI's audited financial statements, the organization failed to include their value in the accounting of compensation to officers and directors contained in its IRS Form 990s.

## PUBLICATIONS AND COMMUNICATION

Periodicals produced by HLI include:

*HLI Reports* (a monthly newsletter for the international prolife movement);

*Fr. Marx's Special Report* (a monthly personal account of Fr. Marx's global journeys, heavily oriented toward raising funds for international programs);

*PRI Review* (bimonthly "debunking anti–life population propaganda and statistics");

*¡Escoge La Vida!*;

*Seminarians for Life International Newsletter* (quarterly);

*Pro–life/family Parish Notes* (monthly resource with bulletin inserts, petitions, homily topics);

*Caminos de Esperanza;* and

*HLPL News.*

Claims 1.5 million readers for its newsletters; reports shipments of prolife and "pro–family" materials to 111 countries.

Also offers publication catalogues in English, French and Spanish, and a "free sample packet" for parish book racks. Publications offered press a wide range of right–wing causes not directly related to abortion or family planning. Titles include:

• *Sex Education: The Final Plague* ("how modern sex education, both modern and 'Catholic', is destroying youth, families, church and society");
• *The Feminist Takeover* (on feminism's "diabolical history and future plans");
• *Ungodly Rage: The Hidden Face of Catholic Feminism;*
• *New World Order: The Ancient Plan of Secret Societies* ("new schemes to bring mankind under one world government"); and
• "How Daycarism Destroyed a Nation" (on "Sweden's sex experience").

## POLICIES AND ACTIVITIES

Founded in Washington, DC in 1981 as the "umbrella organization" for Fr. Marx's "pro– life" work, HLI is an organization which has wedded one man's charisma to an international movement.

HLI works closely with key members of the hierarchy around the world. Cardinal Alfonso Lopez–Trujillo, President of the Pontifical Commission on the Family, has spoken at HLI events on more than one occasion. HLI has been welcomed to Holland by Cardinal Adrianus Simonis of

Utrecht, has cosponsored at least one event with the Kenyan Catholic Conference and boasts of close ties with ordinaries throughout Latin America. Bishop Austin Vaughan of New York and other US activist bishops participate in HLI events regularly.[20]

### Policies

"Pro–life and pro–family" are HLI's watchwords, but Marx and his associates stretch these terms to cover a very wide range of goals.

On the traditional defining issues of the prolife movement — abortion, euthanasia, family planning — HLI is distinguished from less sectarian groups by the extent to which it takes an explicitly Roman Catholic approach and by its aggressive intolerance for dissenting views. It explicitly follows "an orthodox Catholic perspective" which emphasizes the "spiritual dimension" of the cause. For Marx, this means that abortion is merely one among many "symptom(s) of sex–run–loose" which must be combatted. He argues that "the roots of baby–killing" lie in "fornication/adultery, contraception and abortifacients" and that "foresight contraception leads to hindsight abortion."[21]

### On sexuality and reproductive issues

**Abortion:** "Since the unborn baby is an innocent 'third party' there can never be any justification for taking his or her life, even in so–called 'hard cases' (rape or incest). In the rare instance where the life of the mother is threatened, a doctor must try to save the life of both mother and child....The cheapening of human life brought about through legalized abortion leads to infanticide and widespread child abuse."[22]

**Contraception:** Opposed unless abstinence or based on natural family planning (NFP). "Acceptance of contraception has led to widespread sexual promiscuity and an ever-increasing explosion of crippling and deadly venereal diseases, including AIDS. ... Contraception always leads to abortion, and to increased abortion rates." [23] (However, Marx strongly supports NFP, and argues against those (including Randall Terry of Operation Rescue) who see NFP as no more acceptable than contraception.[24])

**Family structure:** "HLI promotes the health and happiness of the nuclear family: a monogamous loving marriage of man and wife open to the creation of new life and to nurturing and caring for children."[25]

**Overpopulation**, HLI says, "is a myth being promulgated for assorted purposes, including the redistribution of wealth and power. Inefficient governmental, economic and other cultural forces, coupled with ignorance–and sometimes involving malevolent political machinations–are the primary causes of world hunger and environmental damage."[26] This stance is very similar to that taken by many progressive organizations involved in international development. However, a review of HLI's activities and publications suggests that the group does little or nothing to translate this rhetoric into action. HLI not only avoids any positive action in support of redistribution of

*Human Life International, continued*

wealth and power in the developing world; on occasion (see discussion of HLI's stands on South Africa below) it has even launched harsh red–baiting attacks against both religious and secular groups which promote fundamental economic change.

**Sex education:** Opposed to all classroom programs, including "what are called abstinence or chastity programs," because "sex ed preoccupies the student with the notion that he is 'sexual,' teaches him an inordinate love of self, and instills personal 'choice' behavior."

**Sterilization:** "Mutilation of the body designed to stop the functioning of a healthy human organ.... used genocidally in Third World nations and against certain racial and ethnic groups in all developed countries."[27]

*On other issues*

HLI literature describes a world riddled with threats to the family, among them day care, feminism, freemasonry, the occult, rock music and the UN Convention on the Rights of the Child. It uses extremely elastic definitions of the threats to life and family, and has redefined a wide range of right–wing economic and political goals as prolife causes.

Marx has said that the Canadian Bishops Conference must have had "a grievous misunderstanding" when it issued an endorsement for UNICEF's work in 1992, since "surely, the Canadian bishops do not wish to be on record endorsing an agency that promotes funding of abortifacients and sterilizations, and abortion advocacy in Third World countries."[28] He called on Canadian bishops to publicly and unequivocally withdraw all support from UNICEF and its programs and — following a $3,000 Vatican donation to support the World Summit for Children — called for a withdrawal of all Catholic church funding of UNICEF.

In the post–Cold War world, HLI sees Protestant fundamentalism, western secularism, and even a supposedly still–potent Communism as enemies which must be defeated. Marx's newsletters have, for example, emphasized the need to:
• "Re–educate Western Europe to help fulfill Pope John Paul II's dream of a re–Christianized, united Europe from the Atlantic to the Urals"
• "Be prepared for great opportunities that could arise, such as Mary's overthrow of Communism in Red China, Cuba, Albania, North Korea and Vietnam."
• Counter competition in eastern Europe from "the sects [which] have moved into Russia *en masse*. Active are the wealthy Sun Myung Moon's Unification Church; followers of evangelists Pat Robertson and Jimmy Swaggart (present on abundant videos); the Hare Krishnas; the Seventh–Day

Adventists; Campus Crusade for Christ; the hippie–like Children of God; and the Mormons. If I forgot any, assume they're there. ... The many Catholic catechists in our audiences told us the sects have the latest audiovisual equipment and sophisticated slides, videos and films, but the catechists have next to nothing."[29]

In Marx's world, even the struggle against South African apartheid was a threat to Catholic and Christian values. In 1987, for example, he quoted approvingly from an HLI–South Africa leader's condemnation of the breakdown of "moral structures that the Christians, particularly the Calvinists, have built up over hundreds of years" and warning that "Nelson Mandela and his Communist Party colleagues" will repeal existing abortion laws and fund birth control programs.[30]

Within the church, Marx joined other members of the radical wing of the anti–abortion movement in condemning "softness" on the part of their more moderate allies. He therefore joined groups like **Pro-Life Action League** in denouncing the **Knights of Columbus**'s failure to expel prochoice politicians and in organizing alumni to withhold contributions from Georgetown University over the recognition of a prochoice student group.[31] He likewise criticized South African bishops for funding the anti–apartheid *New Nation*, a newspaper which has served as the leading voice for efforts to achieve a racially equitable redistribution of wealth and power in South Africa.[32]

PEOPLE

*Officers*
Marx, Fr. Paul, OSB, Founder and President
Lalonde, Robert A., Vice–President
Laubach, Father Barnabas, OSB, San Bernadino, CA, Secretary
LaPalm, Michele
Llaguno, Magaly, Miami, FL, Treasurer

*Senior Staff*
Habiger, Rev. Matthew, OSB, President HLI Canada and Executive Director HLI
Guilfoyle, Jean M., Director, Population Research Institute
Kirby, Vernon, Director of Publications
Marshner, William, Editor, *HLI Reports* [See **Christendom College**]

Total staff 50 people, including 25 in Washington

# KNIGHTS OF COLUMBUS

*Supreme Office:*
*One Columbus Plaza,*
*New Haven, CT 06510–3326*
*Tel: 203–772–2130*
*Fax: 203–773–7000*

*Washington Office:*
*1275 Pennsylvania Avenue NW, Suite 501*
*Washington, DC 20004–2404*
*202–628–2355*

## MEMBERSHIP, STRUCTURE, FINANCES

### Membership

As of June 30, 1993 the all–male **Knights of Columbus** claimed 1,534,409 members, of whom 507,948 were "insurance members" and 1,026,461 were "associate members." It calls itself "the world's largest organization of Catholic laity."[33]

### Chapters and branches

As of 1993, it had 10,186 local units, known as councils, located in the United States, Canada, Mexico and the Philippines. Membership is growing fastest in the Philippines; it is slowly declining in the United States.

### Financial data[34]

Financially speaking, the Knights of Columbus is a fast–growing, moderately large insurance company attached to a Catholic fraternal order. With $4.4 billion in assets, the Knights of Columbus ranks among the 100 largest of North America's more than 1,000 insurance companies. Over the past decade, it has enjoyed growth rates far higher than the industry average, with insurance in force up 194 percent; premium income up 357 percent; and total income up 282 percent. It employs more than 1,300 insurance sales people. Other key financial facts about this highly profitable business venture include (as of 1992) the following:

- Earnings on investments: $311 million (7% of assets)
- Premium income: $629 million
- $22.2 billion worth of insurance in force, and $951 million in annuities on deposit at year's end.

For the most part, the Knights' insurance arm holds the same types of assets as any other insurance company: bonds, common stock, and commercial or residential mortgages.

However, this insurance company also serves as mortgage banker to the Catholic church. Over the past 13 years, the Knights provided 237 mortgage loans totalling $212 million to Catholic dioceses, parishes and other Catholic religious institutions. Church loans outstanding totalled $84 million (about 2 percent of total assets) at the end of 1992. Church borrowers have received preferential treatment; the Knights periodically provide cost–free refinancing of older, high interest rate loans to Catholic institutions.

The Knights are also a non–profit charitable organization which receives more than $90 million in tax deductible donations annually, and channels those funds to a variety of religious, educational and social activities. The organization has a group tax exemption which covers its local affiliates as well as the national organization.

In 1992, the Knights spent a reported $93 million on charitable activities. Only $2.74 million was specifically allocated to prolife programs, but this figure appears to not include general support for Catholic dioceses, parishes, hospitals, clinics, schools and other church–controlled institutions which devote portions of their general revenue to anti–abortion organizing, natural family planning or other prolife activities.

Canada looms disproportionately large as a source of funds for these activities. It is impossible to find out the precise proportion of funding which comes from Canadian affiliates, since the Knights do not publish a full geographic breakdown of donations. However, they do give per capita and total figures for the highest–contributing US states and Canadian provinces which contribute most generously. These listings show that members in Ontario give more than Knights anywhere else. In 1992, they gave $7.7 million, more than 8 percent of all contributions by local affiliates.

One key set of facts, the salaries paid to top leaders of the Knights, is omitted from the otherwise comprehensive financial report provided to members. But a 1991 study of Knights finances, compiled from insurance regulatory records in several states, revealed that Supreme Knight Virgil Dechant was paid $455,500 in 1991. That year's total salary and benefits bills for the top 10 Knights' directors totalled $1.7 million. In 1990, the organization spent $2.7 million on leaders' travel expenses.[35] Four other officers were paid more than $100,000.[36]

For at least the past three years, the Knights have been the leading funder of **USCC/NCCB** prolife activity, providing $5 million in cash donations and $1 million in kind in 1990–92. They also provided substantial funding to the anti–abortion work of the Canadian and Mexican bishops' conferences, and to the prolife work of other groups, including Birthright and Pro–Life Athletes Inc.

Political spending by the national organization and local chapters in 1992 included $450,000 for a failed 1992 anti–abortion referendum in Maryland and $200,000 for a successful campaign against a California assisted suicide referendum.

Planned prolife funding commitments for 1993 included:

- $200,000 for public relations services of Capitoline Inc., which succeeded Hill and Knowlton (also funded primarily

*Knights of Columbus, continued*

by the Knights) as the firm handling the USCC's antichoice public relations work;

- $ 45,000 for prolife advertising and publication of the monthly newsletter *Life Insight* by the USCC;
- $125,000 to support Helen Alvaré as the NCCB's prolife spokesperson;
- $150,000 for USCC/NCCB natural family planning (NFP) programs;
- $156,000 for the Canadian bishops' NFP program;
- $100,000 for a prolife film that premiered at World Youth Day in Denver; and
- Unspecified funding of a USCC prolife postcard campaign which generated more than six million postcard to legislators on "Pro–Life Sunday 1993."

The Knights also make substantial direct grants to the pope and the Vatican. They provided the pope with $2 million in 1992 (and a total of $16.2 million since 1981) for his personal charities. They pay for the Vatican's TV satellite uplink and funded the opening of a North American campus of the Pontifical John Paul II Institute for Studies on Marriage and Family. They have financed numerous building projects at the Vatican, including restoration of the facade of St. Peter's Basilica. They also contribute to the Pontifical Council for the Family and the Holy See's Permanent Observer Mission at the United Nations. Supreme Knight Dechant has served since 1990 on the Council of Superintendency of the Institute for Works of Religion, commonly known as the Vatican Bank.

### POLICIES AND ACTIVITIES

On questions defined by the right–wing as family values issues, the Knights of Columbus offer constant, fervent reaffirmations of their loyalty to the pope and his bishops, and closely follow the policy positions of the US Catholic Conference/National Conference of Catholic Bishops. On the economic justice and international peace issues which are also key elements of the US bishops' public policy agenda (See USCC/NCCB listing) they say nothing.

The Knights' selective approach to church teachings is well reflected by the public policy–related resolutions adopted at their 1993 convention,[37] which opened with a mass concelebrated by almost 50 bishops:

- In a resolution on the "Crusade for Life," the Knights affirmed their opposition to legal abortion and public funding of abortions and "deplored" Clinton administration policies on fetal tissue research, RU–486, abortion referrals at federal family planning clinics, and foreign aid support for abortion;
- A resolution on *Humanae Vitae* reaffirmed their support for papal teachings banning contraception;
- A resolution on "Decency in Media" condemned "pornography ... graphic violence [and] hostile and contemptuous" treatment of the Catholic church in the news media; called

for adoption "as needed" of new legislation "governing the content and practice of the media"; and endorsed the work of "organizations like Morality in Media, Citizens for Decency, Canadians for Decency and Alianza Nacional Para la Defensa de la Moral Familiar;"
- A resolution on education called for adoption of school voucher programs or other means to aid families with children in non–public schools; denounced school–based abortion counseling and contraceptive distribution; and
- On presidential appointments, they called for President Clinton to withdraw the nomination of Joycelyn Elders as Surgeon General.

This truncated view of Catholic social teachings leads Knights leadership into the Republican camp. Their 1992 meeting offered an especially blatant display of partisanship, complete with a campaign speech by President Bush and private meetings for the president with Cardinal John O'Connor and Supreme Knight Dechant. The Knights enthusiastically applauded Bush's antichoice rhetoric, his attacks on Clinton's record, and his calls for school prayer and government aid to parochial schools.[38] When Bill Clinton defeated Bush a few months later, Brooklyn Bishop Thomas Daily, the Knights' chaplain, predicted that relations between the Knights and the White House would cool under the new, prochoice president.[39]

Despite their unwavering opposition to abortion and contraception, the Knights, like the USCC/NCCB, were criticized in the 1980s by antichoice activists who thought them insufficiently militant. Not until 1988 did they open their Washington office,[40] which has since become their center for political action against abortion. Like the USCC/NCCB, the Knights responded to activists' complaints by greatly expanding their antichoice work in the early 1990s. Since 1990, when they promised to bankroll a $5 million, three–year prolife publicity campaign by the USCC/NCCB, they have been the primary funders of the US bishops' antichoice work.

Three of the most prominent Catholic antichoice activists — Fr. Paul Marx of **Human Life International (HLI)**, Judie Brown of the **American Life League** and Joseph Scheidler of the **Pro–Life Action League** — jointly chastised the Knights in 1989 for failing to expel prochoice politicians.[41] They argued that permitting such officials to remain members of a Catholic fraternal order was a "festering scandal" which reflected "the Pontius Pilate approach" of Knights leadership.

Though the Knights refused to launch a membership purge (because "we're an evangelizing church, not a punitive church," explained Chaplain Daily),[42] prominent prochoice Knights face increasingly widespread sanctions. The crackdown appears to have started in New Jersey, where Camden Bishop James McHugh pushed former Governor James Florio to resign from the Knights by decreeing that they and other Catholic organizations in his diocese could not let prochoice politicians hold office, receive awards or speak at their meetings.[43] Within three years, McHugh's rules became national

Knights policy, with the passage of a resolution barring prochoice supporters and "especially public officials" from addressing the Knights, holding office, or enjoying any other "honors or privileges of our Order of any type."[44]

The Knights' narrowly–defined Catholicism leaves so little space for other views that press coverage of dissenting views tends to be equated with "anti–Catholicism." "The 'new' anti–Catholicism," Knights Communications Director Russell Shaw has argued in the *National Catholic Register*, "involves giving preferred treatment, in coverage and commentary, to Catholic dissenters at the expense of orthodox Catholicism." The Knights have cooperated with the **Catholic League for Religious and Civil Rights** in sponsoring research and public events designed to combat this Catholic "anti–Catholicism." For Shaw, this new "anti–Catholicism" is epitomized by *New York Times* columnist Anna Quindlen.[45]

Shaw is the Knights' most visible media spokesman, and his network of personal ties provide one index to the "acceptable" forms which Catholic activism can take. A member of **Opus Dei** and a former USCC/NCCB Public Affairs Secretary, Shaw serves on the CLRCR Board of Directors and the **Catholic Campaign for America** National Committee. He is a regular columnist for the conservative *National Catholic Register*.

The selective approach to Catholic social action is also well reflected in the activities of Knights Chaplain, Bishop Thomas Daily of Brooklyn. On abortion, Daily is a militant activist who marches against a clinic on the first Saturday of every month, often accompanied by Msgr. Philip Reilly, founder of the **Helpers of God's Precious Infants**. He has been an aggressive opponent of the New York public school system's sex education and AIDS education programs. Intolerant of theological or political dissent, he removed liberal theologian Fr. Richard McBrien's column from the diocesan newspaper after becoming bishop of Brooklyn in 1990. During the Persian Gulf War he banned anti–war religious services from his cathedral.[46]

## PEOPLE

*Leadership*

Dechant, Virgil C., Supreme Knight since 1977
Daily, Bishop Thomas V. of Brooklyn, Supreme Chaplain
Flinn, Ellis D., Deputy Supreme Knight
Riesbeck, Charles P. Jr., Supreme Secretary
Wade, Robert F., Supreme Treasurer
Donlin, Judge W. Patrick, Supreme Advocate
Ostdiek, Robert H., Supreme Warden

*Supreme Directors*

Barber, Nestor V.
Beck, Darrell W.
Benedetti, Albert J.
Castello, Albert J.
Ertel, Grant R.
Flanagan, Newman A.
Garcia, Ricardo H.
Jackson, Frank M. III
Lacoursiere, Jules A.
Migneault, Jean
Murphy, James W.
Rivera–Santana, Enrique
Shaughnessy, Thomas H.
Waltz, Michael E.

*Key staff*

Anderson, Carl A., Vice–President for public policy/Wash. office
Shaw, Russell, Director of Publications
Erken, Gregory, Lobbyist

# KNIGHTS OF MALTA OF ST. JOHN OF JERUSALEM INC.

*(Full name: Sovereign Military and Hospitaller Order of St. John of Jerusalem of Rhodes and of Malta)*

| | | | |
|---|---|---|---|
| *American Association* | *Federal Association of U.S.A.* | *Western Association of U.S.A.* | *World Headquarters* |
| *1011 First Avenue, New York* | *1730 M Street, NW, Suite 301* | *465 California Street* | *Via Condotti, 68* |
| *Archdiocese* | *Washington, DC 20036* | *Suite 812* | *Palazzo Malta* |
| *New York, NY 10022* | *Tel: 202–331–2494* | *San Francisco, CA 94104* | *00187 Rome* |
| *Tel: 212–308–3813* | *Fax: 202–331–1149* | *Tel: 415–788–4550* | |

## MEMBERSHIP, STRUCTURE AND FINANCES

Membership estimates vary between 10,000 and 13,000 worldwide, and between 1,500 and 2,500 in the United States.[47] Members of the Western Association are required to donate at least $3,000 per year to **Knights of Malta** charities.[48]

Knights of Malta economic power rests on the vast wealth of its members; financial statements had not yet been obtained when this report went to press.

## POLICIES AND ACTIVITIES[49]

The most regal of Catholic lay societies, the Knights of Malta was formed in the 11th century to provide medical aid to Christian pilgrims in the Holy Land, but became a military order in the 12th century and was a military force in the Mediterranean, headquartered in Malta from the 15th century until Napoleon won control of the island in 1789. It reorganized under papal protection in the 1800s, and gradually evolved into an aristocratic fraternal organization dedicated to helping the sick and wounded. The Knights of Malta says that its charitable work, which has continued to the present day, now includes operating or supporting 200 hospitals and clinics in 90 countries.[50]

Ecclesiastically, the Knights of Malta is a lay religious order whose elected head, the Grand Master, must be approved by the pope and enjoys the rank of cardinal. Politically, it remains a sovereign entity whose "ambassadors" enjoy full diplomatic status in dozens of countries around the world.

As a charitable non–governmental organization with diplomatic immunity in many countries (though not the United States), the Knights of Malta enjoys a freedom of operation unique among international service organizations. The unique status of the organization makes it an attractive foreign aid partner. An August, 1993 US Agency for International Development study of emergency aid needs in strife–torn Zaire refers to the Knights of Malta's Zaire Embassy as "a valuable asset yet to be tapped to its fullest." It notes that the Knights' ambassador "has an extensive network of contacts on all political fronts" coupled with the ability to "obtain diplomatic treatment" for emergency relief supplies.[51]

As a sovereign entity controlled by a handful of wealthy aristocrats and business people, the Knights of Malta also can

— and often does — become a potent instrument for covertly achieving political and quasi–military goals which its members could not hope to attain through democratic methods.

The first of three US branches was established in the 1920s by conservative Catholic business leaders, including Joseph P. Grace, Joseph Kennedy and US Steel Chairman John Farrell. Cardinal Francis Spellman, who was involved from the start and adopted the title of "Grand Protector," established an enduring link between US Knights and the New York Archdiocese.

Before and during World War II, some European members of the Knights of Malta collaborated with Nazism in Germany, fascism in Italy or Franco's falangist movement in Spain. After the war, branches for the Knights of Malta in the United States, Latin America, Italy and Germany collaborated with the Office of Strategic Services and its successor, the Central Intelligence Agency, in an elaborate scheme to smuggle Nazis, fascists and collaborators out of Europe. This operation set the pattern for subsequent Knights of Malta–CIA collaboration in covert operations to defeat communist politicians in Italy and support the Nicaraguan contras in Central America.[52]

The political and the humanitarian sides of the Knights of Malta were both much in evidence during the Reagan–Bush years, after a dynamic leader, J. Peter Grace, reinvigorated the group, working closely at times with CIA director and fellow Knight William Casey.

In 1982, Grace and another prominent Knight, former Treasury Secretary William Simon, worked with their friend Ray Macauley to create a new international charity, AmeriCares, which was to become a vehicle for Knights of Malta–backed projects around the world. AmeriCares also won support from the Protestant right: as of 1984, ten percent of its funding came from Pat Robertson's Christian Broadcasting Network, according to Macauley. Founder Macauley, though not a Catholic, is a recipient of the Cross of the Commander of the Order of Malta. AmeriCares advisory committee member General Richard G. Stilwell served as Deputy Undersecretary of Defense for Policy in the Reagan administration at the time of AmeriCares' formation, and was in charge of Pentagon intelligence activities.

AmeriCares' early initiatives included a Central America program which, according to the *Washington Post*, channeled medical aid to Nicaraguan contra backers in Honduras and a counter–insurgency "model villages" (forced resettlement camps) program in Guatemala. In Honduras, the program's facilitators included local Knights of Malta co–chair Roberto Alejos who lent his estates (in 1960) to the CIA as a training ground for the Bay of Pigs invasion of Cuba. A related $10 million El Salvador program was run by a former FBI agent operating from International Harvester's warehouses and used the Salvadoran military to help distribute supplies.[53]

New York's late Cardinal Terrence Cooke tried with limited success to restrain Grace's grand schemes; Archbishop (later Cardinal) John O'Connor, appointed to replace Cooke in 1984, enthusiastically embraced them. State department documents obtained under the Freedom of Information Act by the *National Catholic Reporter* document varying levels of Knights of Malta–State Department communication on projects, including a plan to resettle ousted Philippine President Ferdinand Marcos and aid shipments to such hot spots as Lebanon, Mozambique and post–US invasion Grenada.[54]

These often secretive, government–linked operations appear to have primarily involved the Knights of Malta's New York and Washington offices; the limited information available on the Knights of Malta in California suggests that it functions more as a social group for members of Catholic high society.

## PEOPLE

*Leadership*
Bertie, Andrew Willoughby Ninian, 78th Grand Master (Rome)
Grace, J. Peter, leader of East Coast branch

*Prominent US members*
Anderson, George W. (former Chair, Joint Chiefs of Staff)
Bolan, Thomas (founder, New York Conservative Party; law partner of the late Roy Cohn)
Buckley, William (founder and Editor–at–Large, *National Review*)
Buckley, James (former Senator from New York)
Denton, Jeremiah (former Senator from Alabama)
Dominici, Pete (Senator from New Mexico)
Frawley, Geraldine (Publisher, *National Catholic Register*)
Haig, General Alexander (former Secretary of State)
Hickel, Walter J. (former Secretary of the Interior)
Iacocca, Lee (former CEO, Chrysler Corporation)
Law, Cardinal Bernard (archbishop of Boston)
Lehrman, Lewis (New York business executive)
Martin, Ralph (co-founder, Word of God)
Monaghan, Thomas S. (owner, Domino's Pizza)
Riordan, Richard (Los Angeles Mayor)
Shea, Martin F., Executive VP Morgan Bank (1983)
Shakespeare, Frank (former US Information Agency Director and US Ambassador to the Vatican)
Simon, William (former US Treasury Secretary)

# OPUS DEI

*99 Overlook Circle*
*New Rochelle, NY 10804*
*Tel: 914–235–0198*
*914–235–1201*
*Fax: 914–235–7805*

*Office of Vice Postulation of Opus*
*Dei in the United States*
*(Information Office)*
*330 Riverside Drive*
*New York, NY 10025*
*Tel: 212–222–3285*

*The Woodlawn Foundation*
*524 North Avenue*
*New Rochelle, NY 10801*
*Tel: 914–632–3778*
*Fax: 914–632–5502*

*The Woodlawn Foundation is a US fundraising arm "supporting the financial and material needs of … projects which have a national scope and special importance for the mission of Opus Dei."* [55]

## MEMBERSHIP, STRUCTURE, FINANCES

### Major affiliates

The **Priestly Society of Holy Cross** is the religious congregation associated with **Opus Dei**.

### Membership

Approximately 75,000 lay members worldwide, including 2,500–3,000 in the United States. About 1,500 priests of 86 nationalities.

### Centers and institutions [56]

Opus Dei maintains centers and affiliates in 42 countries, but its greatest strength is in the Spanish–speaking world. Its largest affiliates are believed to be in Spain, Mexico, Italy, and possibly the Philippines. Opus Dei emphasizes recruitment of students, intellectuals and professionals; in some countries, separate branches also exist for workers and/or peasants. Branches are segregated according to gender. It also operates universities in Spain, Mexico, Colombia and Peru.

US cities with significant concentrations of members include Boston, Burlington (Vermont), Milwaukee, Newark, New York, Providence, St. Louis, San Francisco, South Bend (Indiana), and Washington, DC.

Opus Dei schools, youth residences, campus ministries and youth groups in the United States can be found in the Boston area (near Harvard and MIT), New York (including Columbia University), Chicago, Milwaukee and South Bend, Indiana.

### Financial data

Opus Dei is often and plausibly described as a very wealthy organization, but data on its expenditures and income are not available. Moreover, its status as a "personal prelature" — a kind of global diocese — may let the organization benefit from the Catholic church's exemption from public disclosure requirements. Additional research, not completed in time for inclusion in this report, may produce new information on the financing of Opus Dei's US operations or those of its affiliated institutions.

Published sources identify two main sources of funds: stringent financial demands placed upon individual members, and direct or indirect operation of business enterprises. [57]

Businesses in many countries reportedly fund Opus Dei's work. Reports indicate that a single Chilean company provided Opus Dei with $250,000 a month during the late 1970s. Jose Maria Ruiz Mateos, Spain's wealthiest business-man through the late 1970s, was a prominent Opus Dei member who provided millions of dollars. Some reports suggest that, at the time of the Banco Ambrosiano scandal in 1982, Opus Dei agreed to bail out the Vatican Bank and pick up 30 percent of the Vatican's annual expenditures. [58]

Individuals are encouraged to make their wills over to Opus Dei at the time of committing themselves to "the fidelity," a contract for permanent membership. Members are encouraged to practice the "apostolate of not giving" neither alms to the poor nor gifts to friends and family, and to preserve funds for Opus Dei. They are pressed to cultivate the wealthy as potential donors. [59]

## PUBLICATIONS AND COMMUNICATION

Scepter Press is publisher of Opus Dei external publications in the United States;

*Noticias* is the internal magazine for women members;

*Cronica* is the internal magazine for men; and

The *Constitutions* of Opus Dei, the organization's chief governing document, is kept secret from all outsiders and most members.

## POLICIES AND ACTIVITIES

"Opus Dei controls a vast multinational business organization … through its 'auxiliary societies', which are economic enterprises controlled by Opus Dei and run by its lay members."— Dr. John J. Roche, Linacre College, Oxford; former Opus Dei member.

"The most influential — and feared — organization in the central administration of the Roman Catholic Church."— *Newsweek*, May 18, 1992.

"To me, as a university chaplain for fifteen years, Opus Dei's secretive and highly dubious methods had clearly made them seem like a cult operating within the Catholic Church."— Paul E. Dinter in *Commonweal*, March 12, 1993.

Wealthy, secretive, totalistic in its demands upon members, Opus Dei is a shadowy organization which provokes fear, anger, and suspicion among many Catholics across the political spectrum. [60]

It was founded in Spain in 1928 by Fr. Josemaria Escriva. Fifteen years later, he founded the *Priestly Society of the Holy Cross*, a religious order "integrally connected" with Opus Dei. Its first US affiliate, in Chicago, was established in 1949.

Under the patronage of Pope John Paul II, Opus Dei's power and influence have grown enormously. The pope's decision to grant Opus Dei the unique status of "personal prelature" (a kind of worldwide quasi–diocese independent of territorial bishops) in 1982 — and to beatify Escriva in 1992 — were powerful demonstrations of his admiration for this secretive and reactionary movement. Opus Dei's power has further been cemented by the appointment of a growing number of bishops from within its ranks, including Fernando Saenz of El Salvador and Klaus King of Feldkirch, Austria.

Though Opus Dei remains small in the United States, there are signs of a deepening penetration, growing ties to the American church hierarchy, and a network of connections with other important organizations. According to Penny Lernoux, it has collaborated with **Legatus** on Central American projects and "enjoys the support of similarly elitist Catholic organizations that draw their membership heavily from the Republican corporate right, such as the Knights of Malta." Two of America's most powerful cardinals, O'Connor of New York and Law of Boston, are partial to Opus Dei priests and have encouraged the development of Opus Dei campus ministries in their dioceses.[61]

Opus Dei spokesmen stress that their organization exists to form the individual lay Christian for his or her role in the world in conformity with the teachings of the Catholic church, but takes no organizational positions on any public issue. Responding to a 1989 *New York Times* article, an Opus Dei official wrote that "members of Opus Dei enjoy complete freedom in all temporal matters in which they may be involved. It is solely in religious matters that they come under the authority of the prelate... In their temporal affairs, whether in politics, business or whatever, members form their own opinions and make their own decisions with the same freedom that all Catholics enjoy in such matters."

Even on issues which are non–controversial among "orthodox" Catholics, Opus Dei takes great pains to insist that it takes no stand as an organization. A 1990 *Washington Times* report that Opus Dei had protested against the appearance of a prochoice speaker on the Catholic University campus elicited this classic response from an individual Opus Dei supporter:

"I agree with Catholic University's decision to cancel a fall debate on abortion. Debating abortion at the pontifical university is preposterous - the Magisterium has proclaimed the truth on this issue.... [But] Opus Dei does not act collectively. Its members, however, with complete freedom and responsibility speak out individually on matters of opinion and, as in this case, on the doctrine of the Catholic Church."[62]

Such disclaimers not withstanding, Opus Dei imparts, as critical ex–member Roche has written, a common world view stemming "from its uncompromising anti–communism, its fundamentalist religious outlook, its international business enterprises, and its long affiliation with the business and military classes of Spain." These characteristics, he notes, make Opus Dei "very attractive to the far right."[63] In Spain, a number of Opus Dei members served in the cabinet of dictator Francisco Franco; in Latin America, they were heavily involved with Augusto Pinochet of Chile and other right–wing dictators.[64]

In the United States, however, it is not Opus Dei's political values but its effort to exert totalistic control over members — and especially over the young recruits it avidly seeks on elite college campuses — which has provoked the greatest controversy.

Opus Dei participates in some activities of the Catholic right. It is represented on the National Committee of the **Catholic Campaign for America**, and **Knights of Columbus** spokesman Russell Shaw, an Opus Dei supernumerary, has promoted the group's work in the Knight's national magazine. Yet the group's fidelity to the Catholic church is a subject of ongoing debate within the Catholic right, as can be seen in the pages of the conservative *National Catholic Register*. Though the *Register* regularly publishes several Opus Dei members — including Shaw and Vatican correspondent Greg Burke — a *Register* review of a recent book on Opus Dei called the group's treatment of women "irksome, if not repugnant and contrary to Catholic teaching."[65]

Ex–members commonly characterize Opus Dei as a cult–like organization which demands total loyalty; exercises constant control over personal thoughts and action; and demands a never–ending effort to proselytize, recruit and raise funds. Women are organized into separate — critics say oppressively subordinate — Opus Dei sections. Opus Dei schools and residences are segregated by gender.[66]

Parents of some young recruits have formed two organizations — the Opus Dei Awareness Network (ODAN) and Our Lady and St. Joseph in Search of the Lost Child — devoted to resisting what they view as Opus Dei's psychologically destructive thought control tactics.[67] Opus Dei officials almost never deny specific allegations of abuse. They instead tend to use deliberately vague language (vague in that it never specifically states whether Opus Dei acknowledges or denies the charges made against it) to argue that the group's practices are appropriate and even commendable if viewed in their proper religious context. For example, Opus Dei's US communications director William A. Schmitt has complained that critics have taken "a number of innocent and even quite laudable practices in Opus Dei and given them a devious, even ominous cast.... obedience can be made to sound dreadful and personal spiritual direction sinister. Ignoring the supernatural point of it all, a genuine Christian apostolate becomes mere recruitment, small acts of self–denial, ludicrous."[68]

Nonetheless, because Opus Dei proselytizing has also aroused concern among some Newman Center directors, the Catholic Campus Ministry Association has publicized ODAN's work and, in 1992, accepted ODAN as a member of CCMA. Parents and others concerned about Opus Dei can

## Opus Dei, continued

contact ODAN at Box 4333, Pittsfield, MA 01202, Phone 413–499–7168; Fax 413–499– 7860.[69]

### PEOPLE

*Key individuals*

del Portillo, Bishop Alvaro, the international leader of Opus Dei and one of at least 13 bishops who are members of the organization

Schmitt, William A., is US Communications Director

Shaw, Russell, an Opus Dei "supernumerary" (married member), probably the organization's most vocal US spokesman

### ENDNOTES

[1] CCA direct mail letter, distributed fall 1993.

[2] CCA's IRS Form 990, 1992.

[3] National Charities Information Bureau, *Wise Giving Guide*: A summary of evaluations of national not–for–profit organizations based on the NCIB's basic standards in philanthropy, Dec. 1993. Other financial issues also may deserve additional scrutiny. For example, Joseph L. Conn ("Unholy Matrimony," *Church and State*, Apr. 1993) reports that CCA spent $50,000 on a TV political advertising campaign in 1992, but CCA's 1992 tax return contains no provision for such an expenditure.

[4] New York State, Office of Charities Registration, *The Solicitation and Collection of Funds for Charitable Purposes* (Article 7–A of the Executive Law). According to records examined by CFFC during a visit to the Office of Charities Registration of the New York's Department of State on Nov. 15, 1993, CCA had not filed the required forms as of that date.

[5] Unless otherwise noted, material on CCA positions is drawn from CCA publications and published interviews with CCA officials, including the following: CCA *Platform* and *Issues Statement; Campaign Update* June–July 1993; press packets for Sept. 5, 1991 and Aug. 25, 1993 CCA press conferences; "Watch out America — they mean business," (interview with Thomas Wykes Jr., the *National Catholic Register*," Aug. 8, 1993); undated direct mail letter signed by Mary Ellen (Mrs. Robert H.) Bork, distributed in Oct. 1993.

[6] *Philadelphia Inquirer*, Feb. 13, 1993.

[7] Catholic News Service report, published in *New World* (Chicago Archdiocesan newspaper), Sept. 13, 1991.

[8] *Detroit Free Press*, Oct. 1, 1989.

[9] Joseph L. Conn, "Unholy Matrimony," *Church and State*, Apr. 1993.

[10] Peter Occhiogrosso, *Once a Catholic*, Ballantine, 1987.

[11] Conn, Joseph L., "Unholy Matrimony," *Church and State*, Apr. 1993, pp. 4–6.

[12] Statement of L. Brent Bozell III, Chairman, Media Research Center, on media coverage of papal visit, Aug. 25, 1993.

[13] Elwell was active in the founding of CCA, but has not been listed on public statements or officers' lists issued since late 1992.

[14] List issued by CCA, Aug. 1993.

[15] Undated fact sheet, "What is Human Life International?"

[16] *National Catholic Register*, July 18, 1993.

[17] Affiliates information drawn from financial disclosures filed with federal and New York state governments, from 1992–93 issues of *HLI Reports*, and from undated "HLI Branches Worldwide HLI Chapters: US/Canada" fact sheet distributed by HLI as of Oct. 1993.

[18] *HLI Reports*, Oct.–Nov. 1992.

[19] HLI's IRS Form 990s and New York State Annual Financial Report (1990–92), and audited financial statements, 1992.

[20] HLI *Special Report* No. 87, Jan.–Feb. 1992; HLI conference announcement brochures; and other HLI publications.

[21] *The Wanderer*, July 30, 1992.

[22] "HLI position statements." (Undated fact sheet, in distribution as of fall 1993.)

[23] "HLI position statements." (Undated fact sheet, in distribution as of fall 1993.)

[24] HLI Special Report No. 87, Jan.–Feb. 1992.

[25] "HLI position statements." (Undated fact sheet, in distribution as of fall 1993.)

[26] "HLI position statements." (Undated fact sheet, in distribution as of fall 1993.)

[27] "HLI position statements." (Undated fact sheet, in distribution as of fall 1993.)

[28] *The Wanderer*, Apr. 2, 1992.

[29] *HLI Special Report* No. 106, Oct. 1993.

[30] HLI *Special Report* No. 87, Jan.–Feb. 1992.

[31] HLI press release, *PR Newswire*, Oct. 25, 1989; *HLI Special Report* No. 65; *Washington Times*, Apr. 10, 1991.

[32] HLI *Special Report* No. 87, Jan.–Feb. 1992.

[33] *Columbia*, Oct. 1993.

[34] Unless otherwise noted, financial data is from reports published in *Columbia*, Oct. 1993.

[35] *National Catholic Reporter*, Apr. 3, 1992.

[36] Knights of Columbus, "Schedule of Compensation." (Document submitted to the Ohio Department of Insurance, Feb. 7, 1992.)

[37] As published in *Columbia*, Oct. 1993.

[38] *New York Times*, Aug. 6, 1992; *The Wanderer*, Aug. 16, 1992.

[39] *National Catholic Register*, Feb. 7, 1993.

[40] Planned Parenthood report on the Knights of Columbus, undated.

[41] HLI Press Release, *PR Newswire*, Oct. 25, 1989; *HLI Special Report* No. 65.

[42] *National Catholic Register*, Feb. 7, 1993.

[43] *Philadelphia Inquirer*, Oct. 23, 1990.

[44] *Columbia*, Oct. 1993.

[45] *National Catholic Register*, Sept. 26, 1993.

[46] *National Catholic Register*, Feb. 7, 1993; *The Wanderer*, Aug. 16 and Sept. 10, 1992.

47 Lernoux, May 5, 1989 and Associated Press, Apr. 11, 1988.

48 *Los Angeles Times*, June 29, 1990.

49 Where not otherwise indicated, the account of the Knights of Malta's history is drawn from Lee, Oct. 14, 1983 and Lernoux, 1989.

50 *Journal of the American Medical Association*, Feb. 20, 1991, *Catholic Almanac* (1993), pp. 597–98.

51 US Agency for International Development, Aug. 1993.

52 Lee, Oct. 14, 1983; Lernoux, p. 290.

53 *Washington Post*, Dec. 27, 1984. See also writings of Lee and Martin, op. cit. and Lee and Kogan, 1986, for additional information on AmeriCares, see also "GroupWatch" report (undated).

54 *National Catholic Reporter*, Aug. 12, 1986.

55 According to an Opus Dei mailing, Oct. 1993.

56 For listings of Opus Dei institutions, see Shaw, 1982, Kamm, 1984, Lernoux, April 10, 1989, Fanlo, 1992.

57 Walsh, 140–159; see also Coleman, *Washington Post* Dec. 6, 1985.

58 *Washington Post*, Dec. 6, 1985. Walsh, 140–159; Coleman, Jan. 27, 1989.

59 ODAN Newsletter Vol. 3, No. 5, 1993; see also Roche 1982.

60 For Opus Dei's history and descriptions of its work, see especially Walsh, 1992 and Lernoux, April 10, 1989, from which this section is largely drawn. On Opus Dei's recruitment tactics and daily life within the organization, see Farrell, April 17, 1992, and the publications of the Opus Dei Awareness Network. For Opus Dei's response to its critics, see Shaw, 1982, Fanlo, 1992 and especially Schmitt, 1992, or consult the many Opus Dei publications available from Scepter Publishers.

61 Lernoux, April 10 and April 17, 1989.

62 *Washington Times*, Aug. 16 and Sept. 3, 1990.

63 Roche, 1982.

64 Kamm, 1984.

65 Crilly, *National Catholic Register*, May 2, 1993.

66 For a chilling depiction of women's lives inside Opus Dei, see Hawkinson, 1984.

67 Farrell, April 17, 1992.

68 Schmitt, Oct. 1992.

69 Farrell, Apr. 17, 1992 and Opus Dei Awareness Network "Educational Packet."

# PART III:
# OTHER CATHOLIC ORGANIZATIONS

## ALLIANCE OF CATHOLIC WOMEN

*Box 5412*
*Baltimore, MD 21285–5412*
*Tel: 410–252–5737*

### MEMBERSHIP, STRUCTURE, FINANCES

Little data is available on this recently formed organization. Literature distributed by **Alliance of Catholic Women** (**ACW**) in fall 1993 indicates that it is "applying for 501(c)(3) designation as a nonprofit tax–exempt organization."

Activity to date suggests that this is a low budget organization. It has no public office; ACW's headquarters and publications office operate out of the homes of group members. Subscription services for the group's quarterly magazine are handled by **Catholics United for Life**.

### PUBLICATIONS AND COMMUNICATION

Quarterly magazine *Hearth*.
ACW has announced plans to create an action newsletter, speakers/writers bureau, and resource/ research center.

### POLICIES AND ACTIVITIES[1]

This very small organization was created in the early 1990s to provide an explicitly Catholic vehicle for promoting anti–feminist ideas similar to those advocated in the Protestant world by **Concerned Women for America**.

It appears that ACW's sole activities to date have been launching a periodical and issuing a statement mourning the election of President Bill Clinton.[2] The group has also said that it intends to create additional outreach vehicles (including a quarterly magazine, speakers/writers bureau, seminars and workshops) for women who are already involved in other conservative or New Right Catholic groups. Leadership consists largely of women already active in other New Right groups, both secular and religious, among them CCA cofounder Mary Ellen Bork and former **Free Congress Foundation** (FCF) "family policy" spokeswoman Connaught Marshner.

ACW literature says the group aims to:

- "UNITE women loyal to the Holy Father and the magisterium in an effort to strengthen the church."
- "CONFRONT the errors of the feminists who do not speak for us."
- "DEVELOP strategies for defending church teachings."
- "TRAIN women who wish to speak or write for authentic womanhood."[3]

ACW saw President Clinton's election as a victory for "the dominant media culture, radical feminists and special interest groups which are in direct conflict with the Church's teachings on life, family and morality." It said that "the Clinton Administration embraces an ideology which, in many ways, is in direct opposition to the values held sacred by the Alliance of Catholic Women," and pledged that ACW members would defend the Catholic faith against the Clinton administration's policies and "pray for the authentic conversion and regeneration of a country which seems to have lost its moral compass."[4]

*Hearth* editor Genevieve Kineke has said that her magazine "is based on the magisterial teachings of the Church and strives for the fullness of femininity. It understands the vocation of women to encompass virgin, bride and mother."

Executive board member Patricia Driscoll, who is president of Womanity (a California–based group involved in chastity education) and a cofounder of the Alliance for Chastity Education, has argued that chastity is the key to success in campaigns to stop "such evils as abortion, contraception, rape, pornography [and] sexually transmitted diseases."

Marshner, a New Right activist since the early 1970s, has argued that "a woman's nature is, simply, other-oriented. . . . Women are ordained by their nature to spend themselves in meeting the needs of others."[5]

*Alliance of Catholic Women, continued*

## PEOPLE

*Executive Board*

Hoffman, Loretta J., Exec. Dir., United Catholic Women of
America
Weber, Janice R., Assoc. Dir. Women for Women
Driscoll, Patricia P., Christian Womanity
Harkins, Laraine, Financial director

*Associates*

Becker, Dee
Kineke, Genevieve
Lacke, Mary Kay
O'Leary, Dale

*Advisors*

Albers, Rosalie R., MD
Bonnaci, Mary Beth MTS
Bork, Mary Ellen Bork
Kelly, Molly
Marshner, Connie
Shields, Ann Elizabeth
Sullivan, Kathleen M.
Vandegaer, Sr. Paula, SSS, LCSW
Walsh, Genevieve

*Spiritual Advisors*

Ronfret, Rev. T. Donald SJ
Scanlan, Rev. Michael TOR
Tracy, Rev. George PhD

# CARDINAL MINDSZENTY FOUNDATION

*P.O. Box 11321*
*St. Louis, MO 63105*
*Tel: 314–727–6279*
*Fax: 314–727–5897*

## MEMBERSHIP, STRUCTURE, FINANCES

Membership costs $15 per year.[6]

The **Cardinal Mindszenty Foundation (CMF)** was once the center of a nationwide Catholic "anti–communist" movement which claimed a vast network of community and parish–based local chapters and study groups. Today, however, its activity appears to be limited to occasional public conferences, usually held in St. Louis, where the group is based. Current membership and budget are not known.[7]

## PUBLICATIONS AND COMMUNICATION

*Mindszenty Report* (monthly)

## POLICIES AND ACTIVITIES

*History*[8]

Founded in 1958 by the late John Fred Schlafly and his sister Eleanor[9], the Cardinal Mindszenty Foundation is named for a late Hungarian cardinal who became a hero to Catholic anti–communists after he was arrested and charged with treason in 1948. The group has been staffed and led ever since primarily by these and other Schlafly family members, most notably John Fred's wife Phyllis, who was CMF's original research director and has remained active with the group throughout.[10]

Though public statements describe the group as broadly concerned with upholding "faith, family and freedom under God,"[11] militant anti–communism was and remains the group's defining principle even in the post cold war era.[12]

Aggressive attack rhetoric has been part of the foundation's public discourse from the start. Its first major project was construction of a nationwide network of school and parish–based anti–communist study groups (5,000 of them by 1963, the group claimed). Such mainstream Catholics as the editor of the Jesuit magazine *America* complained that these "hordes of misguided fanatics and unbalanced zealots" were tarnishing the name of Hungary's Cardinal Mindszenty by "misrepresent[ing] the cause of human freedom." Charges that Mindszenty himself was an anti–Semite who failed to resist fascism during World War II and defended ex–fascists after the war have been adamantly denied by the Schlaflys.

Foundation leaders have been involved over the years with secular extreme right groups. The most notorious of the groups with which CMF leaders have been connected is the World Anti–Communist League (WACL). John Fred Schlafly's involvement with WACL dates back to 1974, if not earlier.[13] A 1986 exposé[14] documented the leading role played within WACL by anti–Semitic, neo–fascist and right wing

death squad groups around the world. John Fred Schlafly became a member of the board of directors of WACL's US affiliate — the United States Council for World Freedom — at its founding in 1981, and had been active in an earlier affiliate which withdrew from WACL in 1975 amidst charges that the global group was anti–Semitic.[15]

Without abandoning its traditional international focus — CMF's 1992 leadership conference examined the prospects for ouster of Communism from China, Cuba, North Korea and Vietnam — the foundation has broadened its agenda over the years, directing much of its attack rhetoric against "unorthodoxy" within the church and liberal social welfare programs in society at large. The McCarthyite style endures undiluted. At one CMF forum, Phyllis Schlafly denounced a Democratic proposal for federal funding of day care as threatening to "Sovietize the American family";[16] at another she linked the Clinton health plan to a threat of "socialized medicine."[17]

CMF's widening focus is paralleled in the writings and activities of Phyllis Schlafly, who has been the most visible Catholic woman on the Republican right at least since 1964, when she was a key Goldwater campaign activist, and the author of the Goldwater campaign book: *A Choice, Not an Echo.* In the 1960s and 1970s, she wrote a half dozen other books — most of them staunchly anti–communist expositions of her views on military and foreign issues — including, in 1972, *Mindszenty: The Man.*[18]

Starting in the late 1970s, however, when she became the most prominent leader of opposition to the equal rights amendment, Schlafly shifted her attention to women's and family issues.[19] The author of a recent book on the antichoice movement argues that sexism on the right thwarted Schlafly's effort "to define herself as an expert in national defense and foreign policy," pushing her into "the pink–collar area of domestic policy." Victim or not, Schlafly best known as leader of the anti–feminist Eagle Forum, her personal organizing vehicle. She has been a prolific creator of right–wing groups, some of which appear to represent little more than an additional letterhead for use in distributing her message. During the Reagan years, she won some federal financial support, in the form of a $622,000 grant to fund her "Task Force on Families in Crisis" as an alternative to feminist–organized battered women's shelters.[20] In 1990, working with former Reagan White House aide Gary Bauer — a frequent Schlafly collaborator — of the Family Research Council, Schlafly responded to the formation of a Republican Coalition for Choice by creating a Republican National Coalition for Life (RNCL).[21] Schlafly and Bauer were among the participants in

## Cardinal Mindszenty Foundation

a November 1991 leadership meeting, organized by Pat Robertson's Christian Coalition — designed to develop a common Religious Right strategy for the 1992 elections.[22] In the run–up to the 1992 Republican convention, Schlafly's RNCL helped spearhead efforts to keep an absolute anti-choice position in the Republican platform.[23]

More talk shop than action group in recent years, CMF has continued to play a significant role in bringing together old–line cold warriors and New Right social policy activists. CMF public forums invariably feature at least one conservative Republican officeholder; Republicans who have addressed the group in recent years include representatives James Talant of Missouri (a Schlafly in–law), Robert Dornan (California), Christopher Cox (California), and Henry Hyde (Illinois). Other featured speakers at CMF events have included Puebla Institute founder (and **Word of God** member) Humberto Belli; CCA founder Mary Ellen Bork; Reed Irvine of Accuracy in Media; Germaine Murray of **Women for Faith and Family**; and former Reagan administration official James Kay, now with the Family Research Council.[24]

PEOPLE

*Leadership*

Schlafly, Eleanor, National Director (since 1961)
Schlafly, Phyllis

*Council*

Brizgys, Most Rev. Vincent
Brown, Rev. Gerald, CM (Chile)
Crawford, Fr. Robert, CM (Philippines)
Devlin, Fr. James, JJ
Dicharry, Fr. F., CM
Dorta–Duque, Fr. Juan, SJ
Druetto, Fr. Bernard, OFM (Taiwan)
Fahy, Msgr. Eugene SJ (Taiwan)
Garvey, Fr. Justin, CP
Gross, Fr. Florence, OFM (Singapore)
Houle, Fr. John, SJ
Kelly, Fr. John, OSA
LoBianco, Fr. Joseph, SVD (Ghana)
O'Reilly, Fr. James
Palagyi, Sr. Andrea, SSS
Parker, Fr. L.K. O'Praem
Raziu, Fr. Alexander
Repole, Fr. Charles, OFM
Ruiz, Fr. Ceferino, SJ (Dominican Republic)
Teste, Fr. Ismael
Thornton, Fr. James, SJ

# CATHOLIC LEAGUE FOR RELIGIOUS AND CIVIL RIGHTS

*1011 First Avenue*
*[the New York Archdiocesan headquarters]*
*New York, NY 10022*
*Tel: 212–371–3191*
*Fax: 212–371–3382*

*Publications Office*
*6324 W. North Avenue*
*Wauwatosa, WI 53213*
*Tel: 414–476–8911*
*Fax: 414–476–9511*

## MEMBERSHIP, STRUCTURE, FINANCES

### Membership

The membership of **Catholic League for Religious and Civil Rights** is under 30,000, with chapters or branches in California, DC, Illinois, Maine, Massachusetts, Minnesota, Missouri, Nebraska, New York, Pennsylvania, and Wisconsin. Membership is down from a peak of 50,000 in 1991.[25]

### Financial data[26]

Registered as 501(c)(3) public charity.

Reported revenue $804 thousand (1992); $1.13 million (1991); $616 thousand (1990).

Reported expenditures $949,000 (1992); $1.03 million (1991); $785,000 (1990).

Reported functional breakdown of 1992 expenditures satisfies NCIB guidelines calling for application of at least 60 percent of funds to program services:

- Management and general 16%
- Fundraising 2%
- Program services 82%

About 95 percent of its funds come through direct donations and fundraising; Combined Federal Campaign provided $35,000 in 1992; it receives contributions through some local United Way affiliates. It owns stocks and bonds worth $450,000.

After assuming the presidency in fall 1993, William Donohue launched a restructuring designed to reverse the consequences of "recent problems, including mismanagement, funding and even alleged nepotism." He cut off funding to all affiliates outside New York, apart from the Boston chapter and the Wisconsin publications office.[27]

## PUBLICATIONS AND COMMUNICATION

*Catholic League* Newsletter (10 times/year)

## POLICIES AND ACTIVITIES[28]

The League was founded in 1973 by Rev. Virgil Blum, whose main previous political activity was advocacy of government funding for parochial schools. Blum formed the League — for the specific purpose of campaigning against legal abortion — a few months after the Supreme Court issued its decision in Roe v. Wade.[29]

Since its founding, however, the League has taken on a broader function on behalf of the Catholic right, on abortion and a number of issues. It works to legally and rhetorically redefine efforts to restrict basic constitutional rights — including freedom of speech, freedom of the press and the right to privacy — as necessary to defend the rights of orthodox Catholics.

The Catholic League self–definition contains two key components. First, it defines itself as a parochial "anti–defamation" organization self–consciously emulating the Anti–Defamation League of B'Nai B'rith.

Second, it defines itself as a "defender" of the civil rights and liberties guaranteed by the US Constitution, but one whose peculiar definitions of "civil rights" and "civil liberties" are opposite to those upheld by conventional defenders of constitutional freedoms. The League has been active since the 1970s as an opponent of affirmative action, and has recently devoted increasing amounts of energy to opposing gay rights legislation. In addition, its bylaws present the League as defender of "the right to life for the unborn, the aged and the handicapped; the rights of the family to protection against threats to morality, such as the promotion of addictive drugs, pornography, amoral approaches to sex and the like; and the rights of parents to direct the education of their children."[30]

This peculiar approach to "civil rights" made League general counsel Robert Destro the perfect foil for Reagan administration efforts to obstruct the US Commission on Civil Rights' efforts to defend the rights of minorities and women. At the time of his appointment as head of the commission, Destro was already on record as arguing that the commission "would not be missed" if it were abolished.[31] A review of the League's activities in the five years preceding his nomination revealed that the overwhelming majority of legal cases it pursued (11 out of 14 during the years covered) were designed not to defend civil rights, but to restrict the right to choice on abortion.[32] A united campaign by minority, women's and civil liberties groups blocked the nomination in 1982, but Reagan renominated Destro the next year and ultimately succeeded in getting him confirmed.

As a "civil liberties" group, the League defines itself by its hostility toward the American Civil Liberties Union, and by its defense of citizens' "right" to censor or suppress offensive speech, language and actions. Indeed Donohue, who taught political science at La Roche College in Pittsburgh, has devoted much of his academic career to an effort to redefine civil liberties. The author of two books which attack the policies of the ACLU, Donohue argues that civil libertarians' "radical individualism is an impoverished sense of liberty."[33] When Massachusetts passed a ban on discrimination against

*Catholic League for Religious and Civil Rights, continued*

gay students in December 1993, a League official charged that it "will result in both limitations upon free speech and discrimination against Catholics and other religious believers, as voicing criticism of homosexual conduct will be viewed as harassment." [34]

The League lobbied in the 1980s to exempt international natural family planning groups funded by the US government from "informed consent" rules designed to safeguard women's freedom to make knowledgeable birth control choices. [35] In 1990, it joined a coalition of Catholic and Protestant conservative antichoice groups — including **Concerned Women for America**, the **Family Research Council**, **American Life League**, the **Free Congress Foundation**, **Feminists for Life of America**, the National Right to Life Committee and the **Pro-Life Action League** in calling for a boycott of corporations which donate money to Planned Parenthood. [36]

The League also frequently seeks government action to punish people who protest the Catholic hierarchy's stands on abortion and gay rights. In recent years, the Boston chapter has:

- Demanded the removal of the head of the Governor's Commission on Gay and Lesbian Youth, because of his participation in a 1990 demonstration at Holy Cross Cathedral opposing Cardinal Bernard Law's stands on abortion and gay rights; [37] and
- Called for the arrest of a small group of demonstrators from the pro-gay organizations ACT UP and Queer Nation who chanted "shame, shame" during a 1992 speech by New York's Cardinal John O'Connor to a group of antichoice activists. [38]

In other actions over the past year, the League:

- Joined New York's Cardinal John O'Connor in successfully demanding removal of a "blasphemous" ad for the rock singer Madonna from public buses.
- Joined the (evangelical Protestant) Christian Legal Society as amicus in a Supreme Court challenge to a ban on religion-based discrimination in hiring by a Protestant school.
- Filed a Massachusetts Supreme Court amicus brief (jointly with Concerned Women for America and the Massachusetts Catholic Conference) supporting the "right" of a landlord to refuse to rent an apartment to an unmarried heterosexual couple.
- Spearheaded a campaign to brand then Surgeon General nominee Joycelyn Elders as "anti-Catholic" based on her criticism of the church's views of abortion. [39]

Internal disputes have divided and weakened the organization in the years since Blum died in 1990. In 1991, then-president John M. Tierney and chief assistant Rev. Robert L. Charlebois filed suit for breach of contract after they were fired. John Puthenveetil served as president (a paid full-time position) in 1992. He was succeeded in the summer of 1993 by William A. Donohue, a Heritage Foundation adjunct scholar. [40]

## PEOPLE
President: Donohue, Dr. William A., 1993–

*Board*
Eichner, Rev. Philip K. SM, Kallenberg H.S., Uniondale, New Jersey (Chair, 1993–)
Blee, Thomas J. Esq. of Burt, Blee, Dixon & Sutton, Ft Wayne, Indiana
Destro, Robert, Columbus School of Law, Catholic University of America, Washington, DC
Hitchcock, Prof. James, History Dept., St Louis University
Jandrisitz, James, Dresher, Pennsylvania
Lundy, Marilyn, Grosse Pointe Shores, Michigan
Mangano, Anthony, Mount Vernon, New York
McCreary, Kathleen S., Scarsdale, New York
McLaughlin, James, San Antonio, Texas and Old Greenwich, Connecticut
McLaughlin, Paul B., Treasurer, Cambridge Univ. Press, Port Chester, New York
Salas, Frank, Coral Gables, Florida
Shaw, Russell, Opus Dei member and Director of Public Information, **Knights of Columbus**
Whitehead, Kenneth, Falls Church, Virginia

# CATHOLICS UNITED FOR LIFE

3050 Gap Knob Road
New Hope, KY 40052
Tel: 502–325–3061
Fax: 502–325–3091

Affiliate, Free Speech Advocates (FSA)
6375 New Hope Rd.
New Hope, KY 40052
Tel: 502–549–5454
Fax: 502–549–5252

Local groups, often parish–based, exist in
Washington, DC and other cities.

## MEMBERSHIP, STRUCTURE FINANCES

**Catholics United for Life** (**CUL**) has no dues–paying membership; it reports that its mailing list includes 20,000 people.[41]

### Financial data

Registered as 501(c)(3) public charity.

Reported revenue of $311 thousand and expenditures of $312 thousand in 1992, the latest year for which IRS Form 990 was available. Functional division of 1992 expenditures was as follows:

- Management and general expense:          10%
- Fundraising (professional fundraising fees):          0%
- Program services:          80%

Revenue fell to a five year low in 1992; peak revenue was $381,302 in 1989.[42]

As described on the 1992 Form 990, CUL's expenditure pattern conforms to the NCIB voluntary guidelines indicating that groups should "spend at least 60% of annual expenses for program activities."[43]

However, CUL's financial relationship with the law firm of Thomas P. Monaghan, the co–chairman of its FSA affiliate (not to be confused with Thomas S. Monaghan of Domino's Pizza and Legatus), appears to contradict claims made in fundraising literature. The literature asserts that "we don't pay officers or a wealthy board of directors — all of our workers volunteer their time as a sacrifice for God's children."[44] However, the organization's Form 990s show that the bulk of its fundraising revenue is paid as "retainer fees" to the law firm of FSA Co–chair Thomas P. Monaghan. In 1992, Monaghan's law firm received a retainer of $180 thousand, almost 60 percent of total CUL receipts. Payments to the Monaghan firm totalled $243 thousand in 1991 and $182 thousand in 1990.[45] A directory assistance inquiry further revealed that FSA and Monaghan's law office are located at the same address.

## PUBLICATIONS AND COMMUNICATION

Newsletter: *Catholics United for Life.*

CUL claims to have produced and distributed in 1992 250 thousand books, pamphlets and leaflets, including charismatic Catholic religious tracts (e.g. "The Third Order, a garden of mystical delight for the laity and secular clergy") as well as anti–abortion, anti–contraception, and pro–abstinence materials.[46]

## POLICIES AND ACTIVITIES

CUL was formed in the 1970s by members of the St. Martin de Porres Lay Dominican Community,[47] and the two groups continue to maintain interlocking leadership. Though it calls itself "the only grass roots Catholic pro–life group in the world,"[48] CUL headquarters functions as a small cadre of leaders and resource people, not a mass organization. It serves as a logistical center for the Rescue Movement and other Catholic right causes. Its printing and mailing list fulfillment services are used by anti–abortion groups and conservative publications (including Hearth, published by the **Alliance of Catholic Women**). CUL does have some parish–based chapters, but they appear to be relatively small in number.

CUL, like the St. Martin de Porres community, is organized as a Third Order (lay) Dominican community, with Theo Stearns as Prioress and Fr. Arthur Klyber as resident chaplain. Its motto is "Jesus Christ, Victor." President Elasah Drogin says she is a convert from Judaism who herself had an abortion before joining the Catholic faith and pledging her "obedience to the Holy Father."[49]

The group is opposed to abortion, artificial birth control and all sexual activity outside marriage. (One CUL–distributed line of tracts, originally published by Womanity, advises young women to avoid "passionate petting" and clothing that advertise "sexiness." These tracts call on the formerly–promiscuous to adopt a "secondary virginity" which can be achieved through sincere repentance and the abandonment of all "genital arousal behavior until after marriage.")[50]

CUL (along with Chicago's **Pro–Life Action League**) was one of the precursors to Operation Rescue. The group claims to have originated "sidewalk counseling" — described in its literature as "confronting women en route to abortion clinics and attempting to persuade them not to abort" — in 1983.[51]

Apart from the printing and the distribution of publications, CUL's main work in recent years has been fundraising for its legal subsidiary, Free Speech Advocates, one of the principal legal defense forces for anti–abortion militants. CUL–FSA has defended clinic bombers (such as those accused in a Christmas 1984 attack on a Pensacola, Florida clinic). CUL–FSA co–chair Charles Rice argues that clinic bombing, though tactically unwise, is morally (and legally) defensible as a method for defending human life.[52]

CUL advisor Mark Drogin goes even further in his rhetoric. "The abortionists are the ones who are violent, not

*Catholics United for Life, continued*

the prolife people," Drogin claims, " Eventually, these abortionists will have to be hunted down like Nazi war criminals." According to the *St. Louis Post Dispatch,* when one abortion provider and his wife were kidnapped by an antichoice "Army of God" August 1982 in the St. Louis area, Drogin commented that the doctor should not have been returned unharmed. Said Drogin, "He might have been released without a hand or something.

On most of its major court cases since 1990 — including "Rescue" defense, anti–Roe v. Wade amicus briefs and action to overturn restrictions on religious use of school facilities — CUL–FSA has worked jointly with Pat Robertson's **American Center for Law and Justice**. CUL and **ACLJ** were joined by the **Catholic League for Religious and Civil Rights**, **Concerned Women for America**, the **Christian Council**, and a number of Protestant denomination–based anti–abortion groups in their April 1992 *amicus* brief supporting Pennsylvania's attempt to nullify portions of Roe v. Wade [53]

When they speak on economic issues, CUL leaders align themselves with the far right. For example, co–chair Rice, in endorsing Patrick Buchanan for president, argued that curtailing "runaway taxation and government spending" is itself a "moral issue."[54]

CUL literature also advertises a youth group, the CUL Young Crusaders, which it describes as also affiliated with the Confraternity of Angelic Warfare. The Young Crusaders, CUL literature says "fight abortion" just as Medieval Crusaders "fought to free the Holy Land" as "soldiers of the cross of Jesus Christ." The Angelic Warfare Confraternity — a Dominican "Third Order" — exists to help these fighters "remain chaste and pure." It must be noted, however, that — outside the dramatic language used in CUL literature — we have been unable to find references to actions of any kind undertaken by the youth wing.[55]

PEOPLE

Drogin, Elasah, TOP, President
Klyber, Fr. Arthur, CSR, Resident Chaplain
Mendoza, Anthony, Vice–President
Stearns, Judy, Secretary
Musk, Dennis J., Treasurer

*CUL Advisors*

Hastrich, Bishop Jerome J. (former Bishop of Gallup, New Mexico, retired 1990)
Olifer, Bishop Fremont Torres
Pursley, Bishop Leo (former Bishop of Fort Wayne, Indiana, resigned 1976)
Drogin, Mark

*FSA leadership*

Rice, Prof. Charles E., University of Notre Dame, co–chair
Monaghan, Thomas Patrick, New Hope, co–chair (and legal staff member)

*FSA Advisory Committee members*

Wallenfang, Ronald L., Milwaukee, Wisconsin
Laird, Michael J., Chicago, Illinois
Smith, William J., Bardstown, Kentucky
Pimentel, Hugh, TOP, Prior, St. Martin de Porres Lay Dominican Community, New Hope Kentucky

*FSA Legal Staff*

Sekulow, Jay Allen, Litigation Counsel
Cornell, C. Peter Thomas S.
Weber, Walter M.
Murphy, James E.

# CATHOLICS UNITED FOR THE FAITH INC.

*50 Washington Avenue*
*New Rochelle, NY 10801*
*Tel: 914–235–9404*
*Fax: 914–235–6106*

## MEMBERSHIP, STRUCTURE, FINANCES

### Membership

**Catholics United for the Faith** (**CUF**) report worldwide membership of 23,000.[56] Though members are scattered across the United States, the most active chapters are located in the Northeast.

Overseas, CUF has national branches in:

• Australia, George Cook, Director
• New Zealand, Melda Townsely, Director

Also reports existence of chapters in Canada and Southeast Asia.

### Financial data [57]

Registered as 501(c)(3) public charity. Revenue $575 thousand in 1992–93 fiscal year; averaged about $450 thousand annually in previous four years.

Functional division of expenditures was as follows:

• Management and general expense      20%
• Fundraising (professional fundraising fees)    12%
• Program services      68%[57]

This expenditure pattern meets voluntary guidelines established by NCIB.[58]

## PUBLICATIONS AND COMMUNICATION

*Lay Witness*, a glossy monthly "to assist in the spiritual and doctrinal formation of the laity;"

*CUF Bulletin*, a 4–pp newsletter on CUF doings;

The *Faith and Life Series*, a Catholic curriculum for grades 1–8;

Operates a books and publications service and an information and documentation service.

## POLICIES AND ACTIVITIES

CUF was founded in 1968 by the late New York stockbroker H. Lyman Stebbins (1911– 1989) to combat those trends within the Catholic church which he viewed as unorthodox. The group's mindset is well captured by a letter in which Stebbins told two of his early supporters "we are surrounded by enemies whom we have a duty to resist; but there is the question of how to engage in all–out warfare fighting under the banner of the Prince of Peace. We are surrounded by bishops who are often failing tragically in their duty to defend and hand on 'the faith that comes to us from the apostles.'"[59]

CUF remained a fringe group of limited influence until Pope John Paul II appointed ultra– conservative Cardinal Silvio Oddi as head of the Congregation for the Clergy in 1979, when it began to respond actively to Oddi's encouragement — in interviews with *The Wanderer* (an orthodox Catholic weekly) — of lay complaints to the Vatican about evidence of unorthodoxy.[60]

A lengthy campaign of complaints to the Vatican organized by CUF, *The Wanderer* and the Catholic Center of Paul Weyrich's **Free Congress Foundation** contributed to the Vatican's disciplining of Seattle Archbishop Raymond Hunthausen. Hunthausen's activism in the peace movement had won him the enmity of the political right, but the attack targeted his views on sacramental and sexual matters. In 1986 — after declaring that it was concerned about Hunthausen's attitudes toward homosexuals, divorce, general absolution and the offering communion for non–Catholics at weddings and funerals — the Vatican placed a new auxiliary bishop in Seattle and gave him primary decision–making authority over the activities of the archdiocese. Many of Hunthausen's friends — including Bishop Walter Sullivan of Richmond, Virginia — believe that Hunthausen's nuclear pacifism, not his alleged doctrinal deviations, were the primary force motivating the crackdown.[61]

Other victims of Vatican sanctions, among them Dominican Father Matthew Fox, likewise blame CUF.[62]

Local chapters monitor the activities of the **US Catholic Conference**, individual bishops, Catholic theologians and Catholic church employees for evidence of unorthodoxy. One typical CUF report notes with dismay the participation of a local diocesan official in a Rochester, New York "AIDS forum" where AIDS activists encouraged distribution of condoms.[63] Another broadside labeled the National Conference of Catholic Bishop's 1990 statement on "human sexuality" education as "a flawed document that is in many respects at odds with Papal teaching on the primacy of parental rights and the essential elements of a genuine education in chastity."[64]

The continuing strength of CUF's Vatican connections was most recently evidenced by the appearance of Cardinal Alfonso Lopez–Trujillo, President of the Pontifical Council for the Family, at its 25th Anniversary conference, held October 1993 in Philadelphia.[65]

## PEOPLE

### Leaders

Likoudis, James, President
Sullivan, James, Vice–President
Schwartz, Henrietta, Secretary/Treasurer

*Catholics United for the Faith Inc., continued*

**Board of Directors**
Stebbins, Madeleine F., Chairman
Puccetti, Patricia I., Board Vice–Chairman
Bradley, Rev. Robert I., SJ, Spiritual Advisor
Hennessy, Daniel K.
Kuffel, Joanne
Osana, Zdenko A.
Summe, John J.
Wale, Richard J. Jr.
Wilson, Ann M.
Sullivan, James A., Vice–President and Editor, *Lay Witness*

# CHRISTENDOM COLLEGE – CHRISTENDOM EDUCATIONAL CORP

*2101 Shenandoah Shores Road*
*Front Royal, VA 22630*
*Tel: 703–636–2908 / Toll free: 800–877–5456*
*Fax: 703–636–1655*

## MEMBERSHIP, STRUCTURE, FINANCES

**Christendom College**, which has 145 students,[66] lists 19 faculty members, but does not indicate how many are full–time, how many part–time.[67]

Christendom Educational Corporation is registered as a 501(c)(3) public charity; IRS Form 990 and other financial documents were not obtained in time for inclusion in this report.

Known donors include the Dr. Scholl Foundation, which gave $30,000 to Christendom in 1990, and the **Domino's Foundation**, headed by college board member Thomas S. Monaghan, which gave $13,000 in 1990–1992.[68] The Coors Foundation has also provided funds to Christendom in the past.[69] Students pay $11,235 per year for tuition, room and board[70] and are required to contribute three hours per week of labor for school maintenance.[71]

## PUBLICATIONS AND COMMUNICATION

Christendom Press is the school's book publishing arm.

*Faith & Reason,* a quarterly academic journal, "faithful to the Magisterium of the Church," published by Christendom Press, Editor Rev. James McLucas.

*Catholic Resource Network*, an on–line information service for conservative Catholics, was established by Christendom co–founder Jeff Mirus together with an Australian group.

## POLICIES AND ACTIVITIES

Christendom was founded in 1977 by former CIA employee Warren H. Carroll, a convert to Catholicism.[72] Christendom College literature stresses the school's religious orthodoxy, says little about its intimate ties to the Catholic right, and nothing about the CIA past of Carroll and board member Vernon A. Walters.

It is a four–year co–ed, lay–operated Catholic college "under the patronage of Our Lady of Fatima and under the Lordship of Christ the King." It is "submissive to the authority of the Bishop of Arlington regarding the orthodoxy of Catholic doctrine taught at the College" and "strives for perfect fidelity to the Magisterium of the Roman Catholic Church with a special loyalty to the Holy Father."[73]

Faculty members "voluntarily" make "an annual public Profession of Faith and renew the Oath of Fidelity proposed by the Vatican Congregation for the Doctrine of the Faith." The meaning of the word "voluntary" is unclear in this context, however, as faculty contracts establish that public "rejection of magisterial teaching on any question of faith or morals (as, for example, Pope Paul VI's teaching on contraception in the encyclical *Humanae Vitae*), or of the authority of the Pope as head of the Roman Catholic Church (as, for example, his authority to prescribe the form of the liturgy of the mass), will be grounds for termination."[74]

Non–Catholics may be admitted to Christendom College. Required core curriculum includes religion, six philosophy and two church history courses as part of its "exploration of truth." Students are encouraged but not required to attend mass, which is offered daily.[75] The college's academic calendar lists the annual March for Life in Washington DC, and the school's catalog says the college "charters buses each year" to the march and "the vast majority of the faculty and student body participate."[76]

The school's politics program includes a required internship with a congressional office, political action committee, "pro–life/pro–family" organization or selected political campaign, and a seminar in practical politics (including direct mail, campaign management, legislative research). It thus provides free labor for causes and for members of Congress linked to the Religious Right, and a training ground for future antichoice and New Right activists.[77]

Prominent Catholic right activists on the board include **Free Congress Foundation** officials Michael Schwartz and Connaught Marshner; General Vernon Walters (a former Deputy Director of the CIA) and Dominos Pizza owner Thomas S. Monaghan. Board member Marshner's husband William — who has served on the staff of both the Free Congress Foundation and **Human Life International** — is a member of the faculty. Former presidents Warren H. Carroll and Damien P. Fedoryka serve on the National Committee of the **Catholic Campaign for America**. Ex–President Carroll, who now chairs the history department, was editor of *The Freedom Fighter*, a monthly newsletter published from the office of the Free Congress Foundation in the 1980s to promote support for right–wing guerrilla and paramilitary forces around the world, including the contras in Nicaragua, RENAMO in Mozambique and UNITA in Angola.[78]

Board member Jo Ann Gasper helped craft the abortion gag order, which silenced abortion counseling in federally–aided family planning clinics, while serving in the Reagan administration as Deputy Assistant Secretary for Population Affairs in the Department of Health and Human Services. In 1987, she was fired from HHS, but quickly got a new job with then–Education Secretary William Bennett.[79] She is also the author of a **Concerned Women for America** publication attacking Planned Parenthood.[80]

*Christendom College–Christendom Educational Corp., continued*

PEOPLE
O'Donnell, Timothy T., President

*Board*
Ashcraft, Thomas J.,
Carroll, Warren
Crotty, Philip,
Cuddeback, Chris
Gasper, Jo Ann
Janaro, Joan, Vice–Chairman
Marshner, Connaught, Secretary
McCarty, J. Laurence, Chairman of the Board
Monaghan, Thomas (Chairman and CEO, *Domino's Pizza*)
Morey, Robert
O'Donnell, Molly
Schwartz, Michael
Scrivener, Robert
Sullivan, Michael B.
Walters, Vernon A.
Wrenn, Msgr Michael J., Pastor, St. John the Evangelist
    Church, New York

*Other key people*
Fedoryka, Damian P., former president
Marshner, Professor William, Theology Department

# DOMINO'S FOUNDATION

*Box 997*
*Ann Arbor, MI 48106*
*Tel: 804–971–7644*

## MEMBERSHIP, STRUCTURE, FINANCES

As a private foundation, Domino's Foundation is not a membership organization.

### Financial data[81]

Grant disbursements rose from $157,000 in 1987 to $1.88 million in 1992; essentially all funds provided by Thomas S. Monaghan.

In 1992, the foundation's main income sources were:

- Domino's Pizza,: $1,616,555
- US Agency for International Development,: $250,000
- Monaghan Family Limited Partnership: $100,000

Major grants to Catholic organizations in 1990–92 (including funds committed but not distributed) were:

- Mission Chapels Foundation (Cathedral in Managua, Nicaragua) : $2.2 million
- **Franciscan University of Steubenville**: $967,000
- **Legatus**: $800,000
- Catholic Church in Honduras (Fr. Silvestre's San Pedro Sula missionary project): $505,000
- Escuela Internacional Sampedrana (San Pedro Sula, Honduras): $500,000
- Papal Foundation: $900,000
- John Paul II Cultural Foundation, Detroit: $200,000
- Servant Ministries, (TV production company associated with **Word of God—Sword of the Spirit**): $150,000
- Diocese of Steubenville Holy Family Center: $100,000
- Eternal Word TV Network : $70,000
- Archdiocese of Managua : $40,000
- Ecclesiastical Communications Corp, NY: $30,000
- **Christendom College**: $13,000
- Holy See Mission to United Nations: $12,500
- Institute on Religious Life, Chicago: $11,000
- Cambridge Center for the Study of Faith and Culture, Boston: $10,000
- **Feminists for Life** Education Project, Kansas City: $10,000
- Brownson Institute, Notre Dame: $5,000
- Evangelization 2000, Lincroft, New Jersey: $3,000

## POLICIES AND ACTIVITIES

Founded by Domino's Pizza owner Thomas S. Monaghan in 1987, this foundation is a primary conduit for his charitable giving. Apart from the Vatican and local Michigan charities, the chief beneficiaries have been conservative Catholic causes with ties to the Ann Arbor, Michigan–based charismatic Word of God–Sword of the Spirit network. (For information on Monaghan's views and activities not directly related to his grant–giving, see Legatus.) Monaghan insists that, though he admires WG–SS leaders, he is not a member.[82]

In 1990–1992, Monaghan used the foundation to give almost $1 million to Franciscan University of Steubenville, whose president, Fr. Michael Scanlan, headed a Word of God–linked community in Steubenville and transformed the university into an education and conference center for far–right charismatics.

Word of God–linked projects in Central America have been a primary focus of Monaghan's giving from the foundation's beginning. In 1990 to 1992, he gave more than $1 million to Central American projects sponsored by Fr. Enrique Silvestre, leader of a Sword of the Spirit branch in Honduras.[83] During the same period, he created a chain of Honduran businesses designed to subsidize Silvestre's work and made land acquisitions in that country. Monaghan also cooperated with WG member Michael J. Healy, Dean of the Faculty at Franciscan University of Steubenville, on plans to create a technical school in Honduras. Domino's Honduran projects also received funding during the Reagan–Bush years from the US Agency for International Development. At a time when Honduras was the main staging ground for contra attacks on Sandinista–led Nicaragua, Monaghan hired an anti–Sandinista Nicaraguan exile to run the Honduran program. Though Monaghan told the liberal *National Catholic Reporter* that his Honduran programs had no political motivation, in an interview with the *Conservative Digest*, he described his belief that US failure to support the contras could lead to Communist takeovers in El Salvador, Panama and Mexico, ultimately confronting the United States with a "Soviet client state along our southern border."[84]

Largely through this foundation, Monaghan also provided $3.5 million of the $4.5 million cost of a new cathedral — to replace one destroyed in a 1972 earthquake — for Managua's Cardinal Obando y Bravo. Monaghan offered the money in response to an appeal issued by President Violeta Chamorro after she defeated the Sandinistas in national elections. Chamorro and the cardinal (See **Knights of Malta**) have also enjoyed substantial support from other key elements of the Catholic right–wing.

Monaghan has also provided at least $100,000 for the televangelism programs of Word of God–Sword of the Spirit cofounder Ralph Martin, who serves with him on the FUS board, and of Sword of the Spirit televangelist Father John Bertolucci.[85] Both Martin and Monaghan were inducted into the Knights of Malta in the late 1980s and participated in a January 1989 ceremony which featured a keynote address by outgoing US President Ronald Reagan.[86]

*Domino's Foundation, continued*

Though Monaghan is also a substantial funder of the anti-choice movement, most of his antichoice giving is from personal funds not funnelled through the foundation. (The only antichoice group listed among the foundation's 1990–92 grant recipients is Feminists for Life.) As of 1989, he acknowledged having given $60,000 to the Michigan Committee to End Tax Funded Abortion. The National Organization for Women and other women's groups contended that his actual antichoice giving totalled at least $500,000 in the 1980s, including sizable donations to Randall Terry's Operation Rescue.[87]

## PEOPLE

### *Officers*
Monaghan, Thomas Stephen, President
Monaghan, Marjorie, Secretary
Skinner, Robert J., Treasurer (Ann Arbor philanthropist, described by Monaghan as his "mentor.")
Kanitz, Betsy, Assistant Secretary

# Franciscan University of Steubenville

*100 Franciscan Way*
*P.O. Box 7200*
*Steubenville, OH 43952–6701*
*Tel: 800–282–8283*
*Tel: 614–283–3771*

## Membership, structure, finances

Franciscan University of Steubenville's student body includes 1,800 students from all 50 states and 40 foreign countries.

### Affiliated and campus–based organizations

Human Life Center;
Catholic Alliance for Faith, Intercession, Repentance and Evangelism (FIRE);
Fraternity of Priests;
Catholic Theological Alliance; and
The Language and Catechetical Institute (Gaming, Austria).

### Financial data

Tuition and fees at FUS totals $9,325 per academic year; with room and board prized at $4200.[88] IRS Form 990 and other financial documents were not obtained in time for inclusion in this report.

## Policies and activities

Fr. Michael Scanlan — a retired Air Force Judge Advocate, former Chairman of the National Committee for Charismatic Renewal and member of the Third Order Regular of St. Francis (TOR) — has been President of the **Franciscan University of Steubenville (FUS)** since 1974.[89] *National Review's* college guide credits Scanlan with turning around an institution that, at the time of his appointment, suffered with "a sullen and rebellious student body, declining enrollment, and growing confusion over its academic mission." He gave the school a new sense of purpose, this conservative guide says, by turning the required Sunday mass into a charismatic celebration, organizing all students into spiritually–centered living communities, and "eas[ing] out" faculty members who "use[d] their positions to propagate Marxism, secular humanism, lesbianism, and feminism."[90]

Under Scanlan's leadership, FUS has also become the key intellectual center and meeting place for authoritarian charismatic groups in the **Word of God–Sword of the Spirit** network (cofounded by FUS Board member Ralph Martin and funded in large part by board member Thomas S. Monaghan); and a home base for FUS's antichoice protesters in eastern Ohio and Western Pennsylvania.[91]

The college catalog proudly advertises its absolute "submi[ssion] to the teaching authority of the Catholic Church" and its anti–abortion stance, which is epitomized by its status as the only college known to offer an academic minor in "Human Life Studies."[92] The school tells prospective students and their parents nothing, however, about its role as a center for a cult–like movement (see Word of God) whose mind control activities were the subject of a formal investigation and forced restructuring by Steubenville Bishop Albert Ottenweller.[93]

Antichoice organizing, including clinic blockades, received highly visible and direct support from university officials, including President Scanlan, in the 1980s. In 1987, Scanlan erected on campus a "Tomb of the Unborn Child" where "an eternal flame is a constant solicitation to vigilant prayer." It has become the prototype for similar monuments now being created across the country by the **Knights of Columbus**.

Scanlan and Steubenville Bishop Ottenweller were themselves arrested during a July 1989 blockade of the Mahoning Women's Center (MWC) in Youngstown, Ohio.[94] FUS students and staff members were highly visible in assaults on area clinics throughout 1989 and 1990, sometimes joining with members of the **Lambs of Christ**.[95] Referring to the Rescue movement, Scanlan predicted in October 1990, "I think we're going to see a couple of deaths, a couple of saints and martyrs, before this is over." The following month a Steubenville student was arrested and later convicted for an assault in which protesters kicked and stomped on MWC staff members, causing spinal injuries, bruised kidneys and a concussion.[96]

After this attack, the clinic won a restraining order against FUS. The violent protests stopped, but Steubenville's role as antichoice training ground through its Human Life Center has continued. Former FUS Student Life director Father John Osterhout, is coauthor of a 1993 statement by Rescue activists declaring that use of "lethal force" against abortion providers, though tactically unwise, is "not intrinsically immoral."[97]

Student life at FUS in the words of FUS enthusiast Cardinal John O'Connor, centers on "personal spiritual development ... within the context of the documents of the Second Vatican Council."[98] In addition to requiring coursework in theology, FUS expects faculty members to integrate "Christian values" into their teaching of secular subjects. Students are encouraged to join small dormitory–based living groups which "have a pattern of living that includes group prayer, teaching, fellowship and sharing" under the leadership of a student "coordinator" with direction from an outside advisor.[99]

In recent years, however, investigations of the Servants of Christ the King charismatic community (one of the Sword of the Spirit charismatic communities) cast a new light on this

*Franciscan University of Steubenville, continued*

seemingly benign approach to inculcation of spiritual values. Scanlan headed the Servants community until 1990; other Servants held key positions on the faculty and served as advisors to FUS campus prayer groups.

Complaints that the Servants were functioning as an authoritarian cult provoked a 1990–91 investigation by Bishop Ottenweller. Members were organized into an authoritarian structure within which each individual was subject to a "Shepherd" who exerted authority over the most intimate details of their daily lives. Shepherds told members how to interact with spouses and children; restricted their access to newspaper and TV news; and directed them even on such daily life details as the decision to hire or not hire a babysitter. Wives were directed to show subservience toward husbands, and men and women to avoid excessive emotional attachment to their spouses or children.

As a result of the investigation, Ottenweller concluded that some Servants' practices were incompatible with Catholicism, directed Scanlan to resign from Servants leadership and directed the community to break all ties to Sword of the Spirit's Ann Arbor–based governing body. Though Ottenweller was interviewed in the local press on the restructuring of the Servants, neither he nor Scanlan has ever publicly discussed its impact on FUS. Thus, while it is known that Servants members remain active at the university, the movement's precise current role in its leadership and direction could not be ascertained.[100]

## PEOPLE

### Key Officers
Scanlan, Fr. Michael, TOR, President
Healy, Michael J., Dean of the Faculty

### Board of Trustees
Hite, Very Rev. Jordan, TOR, , Chairman
Yelenc, Rev. Joseph, TOR , Vice Chairman
Beaudry, Marcel
Doherty, Michael W.
Donell, Donald R.
Gentile, Very Rev. Emile, TOR
Howard, Dr. Thomas T.
Martin, Ralph
McBride, Br. Mark P., TOR
Monaghan, Thomas S.
Pohl, Paul Michael
Sanders, Barbara
Smith, Joan H.
Thomas, Robert
von Hildebrand, Dr. Alice
Wiggins, Michael C.
Zeis, Rev. Gabriel, TOR

# LAMBS OF CHRIST
*[also known as Victim Souls for the Unborn Christ Child]*
*No fixed address*

## MEMBERSHIP, STRUCTURE, FINANCES

Neither membership figures nor financial data are currently available for this purportedly looseknit group. According to Rescue movement, the **Lambs of Christ** has no money: members have purportedly forsaken family, property and personal security for a life of total devotion to saving unborn life. One Lambs spokesman, retired "military employee" Ronald Maxon, has told the *New York Times* that the group has three tiers of members: 30 full–time roving activists, about 100 who travel with them for periods of several months at a time and about 3,000 anonymous members of prayer groups, monasteries and convents which support the Lambs.[101]

## POLICIES AND ACTIVITIES

Despite their claims of structurelessness, some observers have noted that the Lambs appear to be organized along para–military lines, perhaps reflecting the military background of many of their leaders. They are predominantly though not exclusively Catholic.

"Spiritual Leader" Norman Weslin, a former Green Beret colonel now in his early sixties, was ordained in 1986 as an Oblate of Wisdom nominally attached to the diocese of Ponce, Puerto Rico.[102] Another Lambs of Christ leader, Chet Gallagher, is a former Las Vegas police officer.[103]

Antichoice militant Julie Loesch Wiley of **Feminists for Life** portrays Weslin as the prototypical Lamb: a widower who — after the death of his wife — gave his house to an unwed mothers' program, entered the priesthood and embarked upon a nomadic antichoice crusade. The Lambs travel around the United States joining or organizing clinic blockades. Their principles dictate total non–cooperation with civic authority: they go limp when arrested, often conceal their names, refuse bail, reject legal aid and fast — though not to death — when imprisoned.[104]

The Lambs have welded clinics shut with metal pipes and plates (see **Franciscan University of Steubenville**, chained themselves to clinic entrances, invaded women's health centers, and engaged in abusive picketing of doctors' homes and their children's schools.[105]

In 1991, they were among the chief organizers of Operation Rescue's Wichita "Summer of Love" protests. They have also joined or organized clinic blockades in Pittsburgh, North Dakota (with support from Fargo Bishop James Sullivan), Houston (during the 1992 Republican convention) and elsewhere.[106]

The Lambs appear to serve as shock troops for — and cooperate closely with — other direct action groups. Rescue luminaries including Republican Rep. Robert Dornan of California, New York Auxiliary Bishop Austin Vaughan and Presbyterian Rev. Joseph Foreman (a leader of Operation Rescue and Missionaries to the Pre–Born) were listed as speakers at a 1992 Lambs' retreat. Lambs leader Gallagher is coauthor (along with Foreman, Vaughan, Wiley, Osterhout of FUS and other militant activists) of a 1993 statement which said that use of "lethal force" against abortion providers, though tactically unwise, is "not intrinsically immoral."[107]

Lambs' leader Weslin expresses an apocalyptic view of the world which extends far beyond the abortion issue. A recent *Wanderer* advertisement offers a video–taped speech in which "Weslin warns the U.S." that "Satan has taken over our government. The chastisement started 22 Jan. 1993 [President Bill Clinton's Inauguration Day]. The Church will go under-ground. His lambs will be persecuted. Martrydom awaits us."[108]

## PEOPLE
*Public spokesmen*
Weslin, Rev. Norman, Founder and Spiritual Leader
Gallagher, Chet

# LEGATUS

*Domino's Farms*
*Ann Arbor, Michigan*
*Tel: 313–930–3854*

## MEMBERSHIP, STRUCTURE, FINANCES

### Chapters and branches

**Legatus** claimed to have 15 chapters and 700 members as of late 1991. Though the group appears to be primarily active in the United States, chapters were also created in Honduras, Mexico and the Philippines.[109]

### Financial data

The **Domino's Foundation** (which provided $800,000 in 1991–92) and dues from individual members are Legatus' primary funding sources. Ten percent of dues are sent to the Vatican. Annual dues are $1,000.[110] IRS Form 990s were not obtained in time for inclusion in this report.

## POLICIES AND ACTIVITIES

Domino's Pizza owner Thomas Monaghan founded Legatus in 1987 as a support group for Catholic corporate and church executives. Membership is limited to private sector executives with more than 50 employees and $4 million in annual sales, heads of major church organizations, and bishops.[111] Monaghan became a **Knight of Malta** one year after the founding of Legatus, and says he joined the Knights primarily to recruit for his own group.[112] Legatus activities — especially in Central America — suggest close connections with **Opus Dei** and the **Word of God–Sword of the Spirit** charismatic network.[113] Though Monaghan has said he is not a member of Word of God or Sword of the Spirit, he has used both Legatus and Domino's Pizza to promote that charismatic network. According to a 1988 study by Russ Bellant:

• Lansing Bishop Kenneth Povish, advisor to Word of God's magazine, served as Michigan chaplain of Legatus;
• Legatus's first executive director also came from Word of God;
• Monaghan appointed a Word of God leader Fr. Patrick Egan, as Domino's Pizza's corporate chaplain;
• A Word of God member ran his campaign for Ann Arbor city council from Domino's corporate headquarters;
• Legatus "integrated Word of God members into its leadership and activities."[114]

Legatus' first chapter was formed in Honduras by Francisco Zuniga, a Nicaraguan who had fled his homeland after the Sandinistas came to power. Zuniga also served as coordinator of Central American operations for Monaghan's Domino Pizza chain, working in conjunction with fellow Sword of the Spirit leader Fr. Enrique Silvestre.[115]

In the late 1980s, Monaghan contemplated withdrawal from the business world to devote all his time to Legatus, but he abandoned that plan after failing to find a buyer willing to meet the $1.2 billion price he sought for his Domino's Pizza company. Monaghan initially established an ambitious agenda of common activities for Legatus members, including monthly meetings for mass and regular international pilgrimages. Though some of these activities have taken place, the group's main impact appears to be its role as a kind of launching pad for another organization that exists to project "orthodox" Catholic values in the mass market for ideas: the **Catholic Campaign for America**, founded by former Legatus Executive Director Marlene Elwell and now headed by Thomas Wykes, former coordinator of chapter development for Legatus.[116]

## PEOPLE

Monaghan, Thomas Stephen, Founder and Chairman

*Prominent members include* [117]
Grace, J. Peter
Kuhn, Bowie
Lehrman, Lewis
Simon, William

# National Committee for a Human Life Amendment

*1511 K Street NW*
*Washington, DC 20005*
*Tel: 202–393–0703*
*Fax: 202–347–1383*

MEMBERSHIP, STRUCTURE, FINANCES

Financial information on the **National Committee for a Human Life Amendment** (**NCHLA**) was not obtained in time for inclusion in this report.

PUBLICATIONS AND COMMUNICATION

Pamphlets including:

• "Abortion and the Supreme Court;"
• "Human Genetics and the Unborn Child," by Dr. Jerome Lejeune;
• "The Unborn Child as a Patient," by Dr. Albert W. Liley; and
• "Abortion: A Help or Hindrance to Public Health?" by Andre E. Hellegers, MD.

POLICIES AND ACTIVITIES

NCHLA was formed as a "Catholic pro–life organization"[118] in early 1974 shortly after Roe v. Wade. According to "Life Insight," a newsletter published by the USCC/NCBB prolife secretariat, NCHLA has worked for more than 20 years "to keep Catholics at the grassroots involved and motivated" in efforts to oppose legal abortion.[119] It appears to have become relatively inactive in the 1980s, but was revived in 1992 as cosponsor, with the **USCC/NCCB's** Secretariat for Pro–Life Activities, of an annual campaign to send antichoice postcards to members of Congress.

In 1994, US dioceses ordered six million sets of four post-cards (three to send to the parishioners' senators and congressional representatives, a fourth to return to NCHLA) for distribution in churches on January 23, according to NCHLA Director Michael Taylor. The 1994 postcards demanded exclusion of abortion from the benefits to be provided by any national health insurance plan. Taylor said 84 percent of US dioceses purchased the cards.[120] In addition to selling the postcards to dioceses, the committee also operates a telephone marketing operation which sends antichoice telegrams to members of Congress at a charge of $8.95 per message.[121]

Taylor has claimed that the first postcard campaign, held January 24, 1993 as part of a new nationwide Catholic parish–based political action effort known as "National Project Life Sunday," generated three million to six million cards to Congress opposing the Freedom of Choice Act.[122]

PEOPLE
Taylor, Michael, Executive Director

# NATIONAL COMMITTEE OF CATHOLIC LAYMEN, INC. AND HUMAN LIFE FOUNDATION, INC.

150 E. 35th Street, Room 840
New York, NY 10016
Tel: 212–679–7330
Fax: 212–725–9793

*The National Committee of Catholic Laymen and the Human Life Foundation share offices and common leadership structure. Other related non–profits are:*

*The Educational Reviewer Inc. (not listed after 1990) and Ad Hoc Committee in Defense of Life (AHCDL)*
1187 National Press Building
Washington, DC 20045
Tel: 202–347–8686
Fax: 202–347–3245

## MEMBERSHIP, STRUCTURE, FINANCES

These are not membership organizations.

### Financial data

**National Committee of Catholic Laymen (NCCL)** is registered as a 501(c)(4) charity; Human Life Foundation (**HLF**) as 501(c)(3).

### Finances — NCCL [123]

Reported revenue of $412 thousand and expenses of $402 thousand in 1992.

Functional division of 1992 expenditures was as follows:

- Management and general expense:    14%
- Fundraising:    30%
- Program services:    56%

This expenditure pattern violates NCIB guidelines regarding distribution of expenditures.

### Finances — HLF [124]

Reported revenue of $494 thousand and expenses of $512 thousand in 1992.

Functional division of 1992 expenditures was as follows:

- Management and general expense:    16%
- Fundraising:    18%
- Program services:    66%

This expenditure pattern conforms to NCIB guidelines regarding distribution of expenditures.

### Finances — common issues

Federal and New York state public disclosure documents show that most of the funds raised by NCCL and HLF in 1992 — the most recent year for which data were available — was paid to members of the McFadden family or to for–profit corporations whose leadership interlocks with that of the two non–profits. Taken together, NCCL and HLF paid:

- $106,000 in rent to Communication Distribution Inc. (identity of owners and directors unknown) under "indefinite" oral agreements; and
- $356,000 for printing and publishing services to Ultra Arts Inc., a subsidiary of *National Review Inc.*[125]

As of November 1992, ownership information could not be obtained for either of these for–profit corporations, as both were in violation of the New York state law which requires the filing of an annual report listing officers and directors.[126] Directory inquiries revealed, however, that both for–profits were located at the same address — the National Review building in New York — as the two non–profit corporations.

In addition, the only identifiable paid officers and staff (both on the HLF payroll) are members of the McFadden family. Faith A. McFadden was paid $21,800 as Secretary of the HLF Board; Maria J. McFadden $30,990 for her work as a staff member. Both paid McFaddens were listed as residing at the same address as James McFadden, the president.[127] Taken together, payments to family members and related corporations absorbed 56 percent of reported 1992 expenditures.

Apart from printing and rent, NCCL's largest program expense in recent years was an annual donation to board member Msgr. Eugene Clark's Church of St. Agnes (total $6,500 over three years). HLF's largest non–printing expense was a "matching grants" program ($67,000 in 1992; $57,000 in 1991) which annually gives $500 to $10,000 to each of several dozen organizations. Most of the beneficiaries of this program are crisis pregnancy centers, but grants have also been made to the Family of the Americas Foundation, the March for Life Fund, and the Missionaries of Charity.[128]

## PUBLICATIONS AND COMMUNICATION:

*Human Life Review*, quarterly journal in quasi–scholarly format, circulation 12,000 (down from 14,500 in 1990), published by HLF; and

*Catholic Eye*, circulation 12,500, published by NCCL; a caustic, sometimes satirical monthly newsletter analyzing Catholic affairs from a conservative viewpoint.[129]

## POLICIES AND ACTIVITIES

NCCL was incorporated in 1973 "to promote the exchange of ideas relating to traditional doctrines and teachings of the Roman Catholic Church among laymen and scholars and to promote research into, and the study of, the doctrines and dogmas of the Church."[130]

HLF was incorporated in 1974 "to educate people of all races and creeds concerning the importance and inviolability of human life and to foster a reverence for the inherent dignity of all human life however threatened or impaired."[131]

Both organizations carry out their missions primarily by disseminating their periodicals, listed above, and other publications. In addition to *Catholic Eye*, NCCL has printed and distributed books or pamphlets by a number of conservative Catholics, including Clare Boothe Luce, Malcolm Muggeridge and William F. Buckley, Jr.

NCCL has, however, also engaged in some political lobbying. The most recent identifiable effort to influence a congressional decision came on the nomination of Joycelyn Elders as Surgeon General of the United States.

"We write to you because you are a fellow Catholic," said an NCCL letter to some members of the Senate, "to urge that you vote to reject the nomination of Dr. Joycelyn Elders [because] ... Dr. Elders has publicly demonstrated bigotry against Christians in general, and Catholics in particular." NCCL warned Senators that it viewed the Elders confirmation vote as "a clear test of Catholic loyalty," and intended to "make every effort" to inform Catholic voters about the response of Catholic Senators to this "test."[132]

Boards and other leadership bodies include a number of well-known figures on the old right. NCCL Counsel Thomas A. Bolan, is a founder of New York's Conservative Party and was law partner of the late Roy Cohn; Richard V. Allen, a Catholic Campaign for America National Committee member, was Ronald Reagan's first National Security Advisor; Priscilla Buckley is a senior editor of *National Review*.

PEOPLE

*Leadership and staff*

McFadden, James, President (NCCL and HLF)
Capano, Edward A., Vice-President and Treasurer (NCCL and HLF)
McFadden, Edward W., Secretary (NCCL)
McFadden, Faith A. Secretary (HLF)
Fowler, John P., Washington Representative (NCCL)
Muggeridge, Anne Roche, Canadian Representative (NCCL)
Bolan, Thomas A., Counsel (NCCL)
McFadden, Robert, Washington Bureau Chief, AHCDL

*Other board members*

McFadden, Robert A. (NCCL)
Clark, Msgr. Eugene V., Church of St. Agnes (HLF)
Teetor, Marjorie (HLF)
Buckley, Priscilla (HLF)

*NCCL "National Committee"*

Abbott, Faith, New York
Allen, Richard V., Washington, DC
Bannon, Dr. Anne, St. Louis, Missouri
Capano, Edward A., Westfield, New Jersey
Hitchcock, James, St. Louis, Missouri
Lynch, Kevin, Washington, DC
Muetzel, Robert N., Columbus, Ohio
Mulligan, Joseph I. Esq., Boston, Massachusetts
Ryan, Neal, Denver, Colorado
Sobran, Joseph, Arlington, Virginia
Uddo, Prof. Basile J., New Orleans, Louisiana
Vitz, Prof Paul C., New York
Welsh, Edward T., Woodlawn, New York

# PRO–LIFE ACTION LEAGUE

*6160 North Cicero Avenue – Suite 600*
*Chicago, IL 60646*
*Tel: 312–777–2900*
*Fax: 312–777–3061*

## MEMBERSHIP, STRUCTURE, FINANCES

### Membership

**Pro–Life Action League** (**PLAL**) claimed it had 12,000 members as of 1993.[133]

### Financial data [134]

Registered as a 501(c)(3) public charity.

Reported revenue of $466 thousand and expenditures of $407 thousand in 1992. Reported functional division of 1992 expenditures was as follows:

- Management and general expense:                30%
- Fundraising:                14%
- Program services:                57%

Even as reported, this expenditure pattern does not comply with NCIB standards under which organizations should "spend at least 60% of annual expenses for program activities."[135] Revenue grew steadily from 1985 ($138 thousand) to 1989 ($517 thousand), but has declined slightly since then.

## PUBLICATIONS AND COMMUNICATION

Newsline (recorded news report): 312–777–2525; and *Pro–Life Action News* (quarterly tabloid newspaper)

## POLICIES AND ACTIVITIES

PLAL was founded 1980 "with the aim of saving babies lives through non–violent direct action."[136] PLAL founder and Executive Director Joseph Scheidler claims credit (as does **Catholics United for Life** — see separate entry) for launching clinic blockades and the "sidewalk counseling" movement. Scheidler supports the death penalty[137] and rejects the "seamless garment" approach to opposing abortion, death penalty and nuclear weaponry as a "specious rationale for naive Catholics to vote for pro–abortion candidates on the theory that a pro–abortion stance can be winked at as long as the candidate otherwise has good liberal credentials."[138]

The organization is built around the combative personality of Scheidler, a conservative Catholic whose flamboyant statements, actions and public appearances are the primary subject of most PLAL publications. Testimonial quotes in fundraising and outreach brochures all stress Scheidler's "leadership" or "inspirational" role. Its literature constantly promotes Scheidler's book, *Closed: 99 Ways to Stop Abortion*, as the bible of pro life activism.[139] Scheidler's hometown newspaper describes him thusly:

"bearded, burly and aggressive, comes across more like Gen. George Patton, the World War II tank commander, than a disciple of Gandhi or King; an admirer has called him 'the Green Beret of the pro-life movement.' ... Scheidler is not at all prayerful, shouting 'Murderers!' through a bullhorn at the staffs of abortion clinics and regularly causing a ruckus."[140]

Scheidler considers contraception "disgusting"[141] and has said that PLAL "opposes all forms of contraception as immoral," and seeks a ban on "those that function as abortifacients."[142]

He professes a commitment to peaceful civil disobedience, but refuses to condemn antichoice violence. On abortion clinic bombings, he has said "I don't condemn them, I don't promote them. What we've seen is some damaged real estate ... It's like bombing Dachau and getting away without hurting anyone.[143]

Catholics who fail to condemn abortion with sufficient fervor — whether pro or antichoice — are favorite targets for his vitriol. In 1991, after he was arrested for disrupting an inaugural mass for prochoice Republican Governor Pete Wilson of California, Scheidler and his associates condemned Sacramento Bishop Francis Quinn for giving "the use of the cathedral to abortion politicians."[144] Later that year, Scheidler (along with Operation Rescue's Randall Terry, who is a non–Catholic) petitioned the pope to excommunicate 27 prochoice Catholic public figures, including New York Governor Mario Cuomo, senators Ted Kennedy, Barbara Mikulski and Daniel Patrick Moynihan, and CFFC's Frances Kissling.[145]

Though PLAL portrays itself as a national and sometimes international organization, its direct activities appear to be largely confined to the Chicago area.

However, Scheidler's personal influence has had an impact on antichoice organizing around the United States. He played a key role in the founding of Operation Rescue and remains a kind of mentor to Rescue leader Randall Terry.[146]

Scheidler was a cofounder in 1984 of the **Pro–Life Action Network** (PLAN), a deliberately loose knit network which meets annually to plan strategies for coordinated assaults on abortion clinics or prochoice politicians and which subsequently gave rise to Operation Rescue.[147] Scheidler often makes public appearances with Rescue leader Terry, who treats him as a respected elder statesman. Scheidler is widely credited with conceiving the leaderless, decentralized structure used by both PLAN and Operation Rescue to evade legal sanctions. In the words of a *Wanderer* reporter:

"The beauty of the P.L.A.N. concept lies in the absence of any leadership strata; it is simply a loose–knit affiliation of pro–life activist groups, each with its own agenda and city base. Hence, there is no national leader who could be inundated with lawsuits and put out of business in short order. The concept called for each city to maintain a local organization, and the leaders would all work together on a particular project if they so agreed. The annual meetings were to provide a forum to present and vote on items such as periodic 'National Days of Rescue' during which we encouraged all direct action groups to participate in some type of abortuary activity, be it a Rescue or a picket with sidewalk counseling."[148]

Scheidler has also claimed credit for devising PLAN's "well–organized, carefully planned" effort "to hound Clinton at every whistle–stop and every coffee klatch" in 1992, and for organizing similar efforts against Democratic presidential candidates Walter Mondale in 1984 and Michael Dukakis in 1988.[149]

Annual strategy conferences are PLAN's only externally identifiable structure. Scheduled participants in the group's 1992 meeting included, in addition to Scheidler, Auxiliary Bishop Austin Vaughan of New York and activists from Good Counsel Home, I Believe in Life Ministry, Missionaries to the Pre–Born, Operation Rescue, Rescue America, Rescue Outreach, School for the Last Days, and Victim Souls for the Unborn Christ Child.

PEOPLE
Scheidler, Joseph M., Executive Director

# SWORD OF THE SPIRIT

*Ann Arbor, Michigan*
*Tel: 313–677–2114*

# SERVANT MINISTRIES

*Ann Arbor, Michigan*
*Tel: 3133–662–8303*

# WORD OF GOD

*Ann Arbor, Michigan*
*Tel: 313–994–3243*

## MEMBERSHIP, STRUCTURE, FINANCES[150]

At the peak of their strength in the 1980s, **Sword of the Spirit** communities had an estimated 20,000 members in 50 US and foreign affiliates. The **Word of God** community in Michigan served as headquarters for the movement.

Members' personal resources provided a large financial base, but one which is impossible for outsiders to measure because funds flowed through so many separate organizations and hierarchically structured "communities." Thomas S. Monaghan's **Domino's Foundation** poured upwards of $1 million per year into projects run by Word of God–Sword of the Spirit members; affiliated institutions (such as the **Franciscan University of Steubenville**) provided substantial additional financing and infrastructure. Required tithing by members further expanded the movement's wealth.

However, the partial collapse of the Word of God–Sword of the Spirit network following official church investigations of its cultlike aspects and its tendency to become a church–within–the–Catholic–church makes it impossible to measure the current size of financial strength of this network of interlocking institutions.

## POLICIES AND ACTIVITIES

Ralph Martin and Steve Clark worked together at the Michigan State University Newman Center in the 1960s, but were fired when the chaplain discovered that they were also working with the Protestant fundamentalist Campus Crusade for Christ. In 1967, they organized a meeting which led first to the formation of the Word of God community then, over time, to the development of a 20,000 member network of charismatic communities known as "Sword of the Spirit."

At the start, these communities were highly decentralized, relatively egalitarian and somewhat influenced by 1960s counter–culture; in the early 1970s, however, the founders began to refashion the movement along rigidly hierarchial lines based on a "shepherding–discipleship" model shared with elements of the Protestant fundamentalist right. (See Franciscan University of Steubenville.) They also joined with charismatic Protestants in an informal secret leadership group, known as "The Council." By the end of the 1980s, many Sword of the Spirit communities required that their members accept the dictates of their "shepherds" on even the minutest details of personal and family life.

The leaders' drive to control every aspect of their followers' lives grew more pronounced throughout the 1970s and 1980s, and brought with it an increasingly militaristic language and structure. There was a growing emphasis on the decadence of traditional churches, the need for a rigidly controlled island of holiness in a sinful world and on the community's role as

God's army against Satan, and the "satanic" influence of humanism and the political left. By 1981, the inner core of the movement, consisting primarily of members of the headquarters community, Word of God, were receiving a special training class to prepare them for this "war." Those who took the course pledged that:

> "We will be loyal to our commanders, knowing that they are committed to defend and provide for our homes and families. We will serve where they direct us in the way they direct us. We will keep our plans and movements hidden from the enemy and his agents."

At the same time, as the network spread internationally, with branches created in Honduras, Ireland, Lebanon, Nicaragua, the Philippines and South Africa. In Central America, and perhaps elsewhere, some members and communities developed links with far right political movements and possibly with US intelligence agencies.

The totalitarian trend took the movement ever further from its egalitarian roots. Internal discontent and, in Catholic parishes where the movement's influence was strong, the misgivings of non–members, brought Sword of the Spirit–linked groups under growing outside scrutiny. In the mid–1980s, then Archbishop Peter Gerety of Newark demanded that a 1,200-member charismatic group in his archdiocese sever ties to Sword of the Spirit; however, local Sword of the Spirit leaders appealed to Rome, where they found some support among key members of the curia.

A more serious backlash developed around 1990, splitting the movement. Dissenters helped provoke an investigation of the group's Steubenville, Ohio affiliate by the conservative bishop of Steubenville, Albert Ottenweiler. Ottenweller's crackdown (See Franciscan University of Steubenville) may have helped speed a splintering of the movement which was already underway.[151] While Ralph Martin publicly repudiated the totalitarian model, co–founder Steve Clark adhered to it. Clark retained control of the Sword of the Spirit structure but some individual communities, including Word of God, loosened their ties to Sword of the Spirit.

Despite its problems in recent years, the influence of this movement, its supporters, and individuals who have passed through it remains pervasive on the Catholic right, especially among those groups and leaders who work most closely with Protestant fundamentalists and charismatics. Keith Fournier, a one–time leader of the Steubenville branch who broke with Sword of the Spirit and publicly apologized for his own authoritarian behavior,[152] went on to become Executive Director of Pat Robertson's American Center for Law and

Justice. William and Connaught Marshner — both long–time participants in Word of God–Sword of the Spirit–related activities, play a key continuing role in the Catholic right's relations with Protestant fundamentalism.

* * *

Of the many Word of God–Sword of the Spirit offshoots, the one which has done the most to conceal its origins and to intervene effectively in public affairs is **The Puebla Institute**.

Puebla's current self–description — "a lay Roman Catholic human rights group, defending freedom of religion for all worldwide... works to stop religious repression by documenting and publicizing restrictions on religious and other human rights, and by mobilizing public support in defense of those who are imprisoned, tortured, exiled or otherwise persecuted"[153] — obscures its origins as a CIA–linked conduit for propaganda against the Sandinistas of Nicaragua.

Puebla was founded in 1982 in Ann Arbor, Michigan by right–wing Nicaraguan exile Humberto Belli as an "action center" of Sword of the Spirit. A promotional brochure from the group's early years was titled "The Puebla Institute: Calling Christians concerned with social justice in Latin America to an authentic Christian response and a rejection of Marxist Liberation Theology."[154] All the group's original directors were Word of God members, as was Belli's then–assistant, Joseph Davis, now a member of the Puebla Board of Directors. Press reports have credibly charged (producing evidence to contradict Belli's denials) that the CIA helped fund, edit, produce and distribute the group's first major publication, a book by Belli titled *Nicaragua: Christians Under Fire.*[155]

Belli later joined the sociology department of Sword of the Spirit–led Franciscan University of Steubenville and in 1990, returned home to lead a crusade to Catholicize Nicaraguan school curriculum as President Violetta Chamorro's education minister.[156] Belli allied the schools with Managua Cardinal Obando y Bravo's drive to advocate abstinence as the sole method of AIDS prevention among youths and obtained a US Agency for International Development grant to replace Sandinista–era sex education texts with new ones that teach the ten commandments, promote monogamy, condemn premarital sex and eliminate information on artificial contraception.[157]

Belli is still listed (as "founder") on Puebla Institute publications, but the group's current president is Nina Shea. Under her leadership, Puebla continued its attacks on the Sandinistas, but broadened its reach internationally, with publications on violations of religious freedom in Cuba, Sudan and China. Recent statements have harshly criticized exiled Haitian President Jean–Bertrand Aristide.[158]

Board members include former President Bush's Ambassador to the Vatican, Thomas Melady, and prominent Catholic neo–conservatives James Finn of Freedom House and George Weigel of the **Ethics and Public Policy Center**.[159]

Under the Bush Administration, Puebla obtained National Endowment for Democracy funding to support "civic education" radio programs in Haiti and "human rights" groups in Nicaragua and among Cuban exiles. But the group's ties with neo–conservative Democrats have helped it project a bipartisan image and may have helped Shea win a place in the official US delegation to the June 1993 United Nations Commission on Human Rights meeting in Vienna, Austria.

PEOPLE

*Key Word of God/Sword of the Spirit leaders :*
Martin, Ralph
Clark, Steve
Scanlan, Fr. Michael TOR

# American Society for TRADITION, FAMILY AND PROPERTY

*Spring Grove, PA*
*Tel: 717–225–7147*

## MEMBERSHIP, STRUCTURE, FINANCES

The American Society for **Tradition, Family and Property** (TFP)[160] is a Brazil–based organization which also lists branches in Argentina, Australia, Bolivia, Canada, Chile, Colombia, Costa Rica, Ecuador, France, Germany, Paraguay, Peru, Portugal, South Africa, Spain, the United Kingdom, Uruguay and Venezuela.[161]

Core members of TFP, most of them youths recruited in their teens, work full–time for the movement. There are an estimated 1,500 to 2,000 such members in Brazil, more than 100 in Spain, 100 in the United States, and 10 to 100 in other branches. The group also has a far wider network of part–time members and supporters. In the United States, the group claimed 22,000 "friends" and distributed its newsletter to 45,000 people, as of 1989.[162]

Internationally, TFP's main source of funding appears to be traditional aristocrats and members of landed elites in Latin America, especially Brazil. US financial information was not obtained in time for inclusion in this report.

## PUBLICATIONS AND COMMUNICATION

Outreach materials often take the form of political or philosophical diatribes signed by founder Plinio Correa de Oliveira, often on obscure–seeming subjects, which TFP publishes as full page, small print, paid advertisements in newspapers around the world.[163] Among the publications currently being promoted by TFP is a new book by Oliveira, *Nobility and Analogous Traditional Elites in the Allocutions of Pius XII — A Theme Illuminating American Social History.*[164]

## POLICIES AND ACTIVITIES

Founded in 1960 by a man who had been prominent in right–wing Catholic social action groups in Brazil since the 1930s, TFP has relatively few US members. It stands on the extreme reactionary fringe of Catholic conservatism, is viewed as an embarrassment by many mainstream conservatives: the conservative *Fidelity* magazine, for example, has described it as an "antidemocratic" cult which preaches a "theology of hate" and keeps its true views hidden so that it can "infiltrate" legitimate right–wing movements.[165] TFP merits a place in a guide to the US Catholic right primarily because one of the most influential Catholic conservatives in the United States, Paul Weyrich of the **Free Congress Foundation**, has devoted considerable energy over the past decade to winning a place for TFP officials in the leadership of a number of more broadly–based Catholic right organizations and coalitions.

TFP's autocratic leader, Oliveira, despises the modern Catholic hierarchy, and has no known allies in senior church leadership. Oliveira aspires to the restoration of medieval Catholicism, looks back fondly to the Holy Inquisition as the church's last moment of glory and is said to view Pope John Paul II as an "apostate." Oliveira's extremism has alienated orthodox conservatives such as the editors of the Ultramontanist Associate's *Fidelity* Magazine, and drove away even Oliveira's one–time mentor — Archbishop Antonio de Castro Mayer — a Brazilian ultraconservative whose own yearnings for the church of the past were so intense that he ultimately followed Bishop Marcel Lefebvre into schism with Rome.[166]

TFP's monarchist, anti–democratic orientation leads it to equate social democracy and even liberalism with communism. TFP supported the military coups which ousted Brazilian President Goulart in 1964 and Allende of Chile in 1973. In South Africa and Namibia it has denounced the Catholic hierarchy and sought ties with the white far right. In Europe, it tries to build ties with ultra–conservative members of titled aristocracy. TFP's branches around the world operate under a variety of different names: including Young Canadians (and Young South Africans) for a Christian Civilization and Sociedad Cultural Covadona in Spain.[167] Critics on both left and right point with alarm to TFP's violent tendencies. A Venezuelan adherent was arrested in 1984 for allegedly plotting to assassinate Pope John Paul II and TFP members elsewhere in Latin America, especially Brazil, have long been involved in neo–fascist paramilitary activity.[168]

Orthodox Catholic conservatives like the editors of *Fidelity* find the activities of TFP especially distressing. They see TFP as a rogue movement which uses false professions of orthodoxy to attract honest conservatives, and then leads them into a blasphemous deification of founder Oliveira and identification of Oliveira's mother with the Virgin Mary.[169] On the political front, they are alarmed by the manner in which this quasi–fascist movement has used a "politically and economically conservative" facade to "infiltrate New Right lobbies like the **Free Congress Foundation** in Washington, DC and ally itself with traditional European right–wing movements like the French *Lecture et Tradition* and the Italian *Alleanza Cattolica*.[170]

TFP's American branch describes itself as "a civic organization whose goal is to foster the value of Christian civilization ... defense of the American heritage, the institution of the family and the right to private property." TFP's quaintly garbed militants — wearing red capes and colorful sashes — are a regular fixture at major antichoice rallies. Yet its medieval and openly anti–democratic worldview would make TFP utterly irrelevant in the United States were it not for its alliance with Weyrich, a politically and theologically conservative Melkite Catholic.

Weyrich made TFP a member of the Free Congress Foundation's **Catholic Center** and has worked assiduously for TFP's inclusion in more mainstream conservative movements. Weyrich's pro–TFP maneuvers have caused dissension on the right, according to the conservative Catholic monthly *Fidelity*. With the exception of Weyrich himself, each prominent Catholic on the Free Congress staff separately and publicly denounced the *Fidelity* exposé. (Connaught and William Marshner quit the *Fidelity* editorial advisory board in protest, Catholic Center head Michael Schwartz filled a full page of the magazine with a letter defending TFP's "faithful[ness]," former Catholic Center head Enrique Rueda launched a campaign to press *Fidelity* board members to seek a public retraction of the article.) "It's not hard to see hand of Mr. Weyrich pulling strings from behind the scenes," *Fidelity's* editors responded, "trying to give the impression that there is broad–based support for TFP when in fact there is none at all."[171]

The Weyrich–TFP relationship has a long history. In the early 1980s, Weyrich helped TFP organized a Washington press conference denouncing Brazilian land reform and the "trained and armed bandits coming out of the basic Christian Communities. In 1986, TFP returned the favor by staging a banquet in Weyrich's honor.[172] In 1989, TFP cosponsored (along with the Republican National Committee and the National Right to Life Committee, among many others) a Weyrich–initiated Conservative Leadership Conference.[173] Over objections from other participants, Weyrich helped orchestrate the inclusion of TFP in several broader Catholic conservative "roundtables" — including the Carroll Group[174] and the Sienna Group for Public Policy.[175] During the 1992 Earth Summit, TFP and Free Congress cosponsored a right–wing "alternative" conference.

Several long–time Free Congress Foundation associates (including Connaught Marshner and *Daily Oklahoman* editorial writer Patrick McGuigan) spoke at TFP's latest outreach effort, a September 1993 Washington, DC seminar. Rep. Robert Dornan was presented with a ceremonial sword honoring his work in Congress.[176] Other "American friends" of TFP include former Reagan administration Central America advisor Morton Blackwell, North Carolina Senator Jesse Helms and former Reagan National Security council staff member Roger Fontaine.[177] (It is worth noting that Blackwell, a member of the Republican National Committee, campaigned against the current chairman of the RNC, Haley Barbour, because of Barbour's interest in distancing the Republican Party from ardent prolifers.)[178]

Perhaps through Weyrich's efforts, TFP Executive Director Steven Schmeider won a place on the National Committee of the broadest conservative Catholic coalition: the **Catholic Campaign for America**.

PEOPLE
Drake, Raymond, President (American Society)
Schmieder, Steven, Executive Director(American Society)
Oliveira, Plinio Correa de, President and founder (Brazil)
Costa, Mario da, Washington spokesman

# WOMEN AFFIRMING LIFE, INC.

*159 Washington St.,*
*Brighton, MA 02135*

## MEMBERSHIP, STRUCTURE, FINANCES

Literature says that contributions to **Women Affirming Life** (**WAL**) are tax deductible. Financial data were not obtained in time for inclusion in this report, and membership figures are not currently available.

## POLICIES AND ACTIVITIES[179]

Women Affirming Life was launched in Boston in 1990 "by a group of Catholic women professionals to offer a pro–life women's perspective in the public debate on abortion."

A one–issue group designed — with active involvement of USCC/NCCB staff members — to project an image of support for the church's position on abortion among intelligent, well–educated, mainstream Catholic professional women, thereby countering the image of a male–dominated church forcing its will on women. WAL has developed a speakers bureau which can provide women doctors, attorneys, nurses and college professors to speak against legal abortion.

It is interesting to note that the literature WAL sends the public in response to routine inquiries — unlike that of other Catholic prolife issues — avoids any mention of the church's anti–contraception stand.

## PEOPLE

Hogan, Frances X.
Law, Cardinal Bernard, Episcopal Advisor

*Advisory Board:*
Alvaré, Helen, Esq. (**USCC/NCCB**)
Angelo, E. Joanne, MD
Bork, Mary Ellen
Chervin, Prof. Ronda
Curro, Ellen
DeLisle, Judy
Dowling, Maureen
Driscoll, Kathleen
Fitzpatrick, Donna, Esq.
Gallagher, Kathleen M.
Garcia, Laura Ph.D.
Glendon, Prof. Mary Ann
Greenwald, Rita
Grier, Dolores Bernadette
Hitchcock, Hellen Hull (**Women for Faith and Family**)
Hogan, Frances X., Esq.
Jackson, Helen T., MD
Kelly, Sr. Margaret John, DC
Little, Lelia Harringon
Long, Sr. Mary Assumpta, OP
Luthin, Marianne Rea
Miller, Amy Esq.
Murphy, Sr. Madonna, CSC
Quinn, Gail Exec. Dir., (**USCC/NCCB**)
Rieg, Carol
Roth, Micheline Mathews, MD
Salvatore, Sr. Christine, FSP
Shivanandan, Mary
Smith, Janet, Ph.D.
Thorn, Victoria
Thorp, Barbara
White, Eileen M., Esq.

# WOMEN FOR FAITH AND FAMILY

*P.O. Box 8326*
*St. Louis, MO 63132*
*Tel/Fax: 314–863–8385*

## MEMBERSHIP, STRUCTURE, FINANCES

### Membership

In addition to its United States operation, **Women for Faith and Family** (**WFF**) has affiliates in Australia, Canada, England, Netherland and New Zealand, although WFF does not have a dues–paying membership. Its publicity generally defines its number of adherents based on a claim that 50,000 women in the United States and 10,000 abroad have signed its "Affirmation of Catholic Women," described below.

### Financial data

Registered as a 501(c)(3) public charity.

Reported revenue of $22 thousand and expenditures of $23 thousand in 1992, and have held steady since 1989, the first year for which data are available. Because of its small size, WFF is not required to give a functional breakdown between program and non–program expense. All officers are unpaid.[180]

## PUBLICATIONS AND COMMUNICATION

*Voices*, a quarterly newsletter

## POLICIES AND ACTIVITIES

WFF was established in September 1984 to "help provide Catholic women a means of expressing unity with the teachings of the Catholic Church, deepening their understanding of the Catholic faith, and transmitting it to others." The founders were six St. Louis women who wanted to counter the feared influence of "alienated" and "dissenting" women on the then–planned pastoral letter on women.[181]

WFF places a Catholic face on the Religious Right's anti–feminist agenda. Its "Affirmation for Catholic Women" — a sweeping statement of belief that "God's Divine Plan" dictates sharp distinctions between male and female roles — is worth quoting some of its key clauses at some length:

1) "We believe that through God's grace our female nature offers us distinct physical and spiritual capabilities ... Specifically, our natural function of childbearing endows us with the spiritual capacity for nurture, instruction, compassion and selflessness, which qualities are necessary to the establishment of families, the basic and Divinely ordained unity of society ...

2) "To attempt to subvert or deny our distinct nature and role as women subverts and denies God's plan for humanity ... We reject all ideologies which seek to eradicate the natural and essential distinction between the sexes...

5) "... reject as an aberrant innovation peculiar to our times

and our society. The notion that priesthood is the 'right' of any human being, male or female. Furthermore, we recognize that the specific role of ordained priesthood is intrinsically connected with and representative of the begetting creativity of God in which only human males can participate..."

On other questions of religious practice, WFF says (in pamphlet titled "Where does Women for Faith and Family stand on issues of concern to me?"

- "Repudiate[s] the increasingly frequent practice of women saying parts of the Eucharistic Prayer with the priest or in his place or performing other liturgical functions reserve to ordained men." Opposed to allowing use of "altar girls."
- "Oppose(s) the systematic elimination from Scripture translations, liturgical texts, hymns, homilies and general usage of 'man' as a generic. The claim that the language is 'sexist' and that such changes are required as a sensitive pastoral response to women collectively is false."
- Rejects all claims that "ideological feminism, which denies the fundamental psychic and spiritual distinctiveness of the sexes and devalues motherhood and the nurturing role of women and in society" represents "the collective belief of women."
- Supports the right of women to choose either to "work outside their homes" or to "decide to remain in the home to care for their homes and families."[182]

On public policy issues, WFF (or Hitchcock speaking in her capacity as WFF leader)

- Opposes abortion under all circumstances;
- Opposes contraception because it "contradicts the life–giving purpose of the sexual act;"[183]
- Expressed hostility toward federal funding of day care and called for greater economic support for "mother's care for her children in the home";[184]
- Opposed the confirmation of Joycelyn Elders as surgeon general.[185]

However, like **Catholics United for the Faith**, WFF appears to devote its greatest to a war of words against the purveyors of unorthodox thought and action, including — sometimes it seems especially — the bishops. One recent WFF newsletter devoted its first eight pages to an attack on the use of a woman mime to portray Jesus when the Stations of the Cross were enacted during Pope John Paul II's visit to Denver. The newsletter includes an open letter to the pope —

*Women for Faith and Family, continued*

signed by leaders of WFF, the Cardinal Mindszenty Foundation, Catholics United for the Faith, Human Life International and other groups — expressing support and sympathy with him over the "deliberate affront" they believe was perpetrated against him by the organizers of this event.

For the most part, WFF speaks with a single voice, that of its prolific chief spokeswoman, Helen Hull Hitchcock. Hitchcock writes for a number of conservative periodicals. Her regular column in *Crisis*, titled "USCC Watch," offers an ongoing critique of liberalism and "subjectivism" in bishops' statements and actions. She closely scours church statements for any signs of softening on women's ordination, "inclusive language," birth control, feminism and other issues.

## PEOPLE

*Leadership*

Hitchcock, Helen Hull , Director and President
Tyree, Sherry, Vice–President
Benofy, Susan J., Treasurer
Murray, Germaine F., Secretary

## ENDNOTES

1. Unless otherwise noted, sources on ACW are a brochure provided by the group; an article in *The Wanderer*, Feb. 4, 1993 and cross–checks of leadership listings with information obtained on other organizations.

2. A systematic review of *The Wanderer, National Catholic Register* and other conservative Catholic periodicals since late 1990 reveals no other references to ACW actions or statements.

3. ACW brochure, in distribution fall 1993.

4. *The Wanderer*, Feb. 4, 1993.

5. *Chicago Tribune*, Aug. 14, 1992.

6. *The Wanderer*, Apr. 29, 1993.

7. Note that CMF has not provided current membership figures for inclusion in the *Catholic Almanac's* survey of Catholic organizations (see 1993 edition, p. 574).

8. The best general source on the Foundation is Chip Berlet, "Cardinal Mindszenty: heroic anti–Communist or anti–Semite or both?," *The St. Louis Journalism Review*, April 1988. Unless otherwise indicated, historical material is drawn from this source or from letters of response (by Eleanor Schlafly and Leslie Konnyu) which appeared in the June 1988 issue.

9. *National Catholic Register*, Aug. 22, 1993.

10. On the involvement of other family members, see also *St. Louis Post–Dispatch*,Feb. 4, 1990.

11. *The Wanderer*, Feb. 4, 1993.

12. See especially reports on the group's 1991 and 1993 National Leadership Conferences in *St. Louis Post–Dispatch*, Apr. 15, 1991 and Apr. 16, 1993.

13. Berlet 1988 (See sidebar: "Fred Schlafly supports WACL").

14. Scott Anderson and Jon Lee Anderson, *Inside the League*, New York: Dodd, Mead and Company, 1986.

15. Anderson, p. 152; see also Berlet.

16. *St. Louis Post–Dispatch*, Apr. 25, 1988..

17. *St. Louis Post–Dispatch*, Apr. 25, 1988.

18. *Who's Who in America* (on–line edition, electronically searched via Compuserve).

19. Women's and family issues have been the focus of all of Schlafly's major works since 1977 (See *Who's Who*). See also McKeegan 1992, p. 21, 30–35.

20. Coulson, 1987.

21. *Boston Globe*, Nov. 2, 1990; *New Republic*, Aug 19, 1991.

22. Conason, 1992.

23. *Washington Watch*, May 1992, *Boston Globe*, May 27, 1992.

24. *The Wanderer* Feb. 4, 1993, Apr. 8, 1993 and various CMF advertisements.

25. Kahn, 1993.

26. Catholic League IRS Form 990s (1990–1992); Audited Financial Statement (1992) and New York State Annual Financial Report (1992).

27. Kahn, 1993.

28. Unless otherwise noted, description of League policies is drawn from the League's bylaws and publications, or from articles in the *National Catholic Register*, May 9 and Dec. 26, 1993. On future goals, see especially the Dec. 26, 1993 Register article.

29. *National Catholic Register*, Dec. 26, 1993.

30. Catholic League bylaws, Article II.

31. Friedman and Nadler, 1983.

32. Frances Kissling, testimony before the Senate Judiciary Committee, Aug. 11, 1982.

33. Kahn, Dec. 26, 1993.

34. Associated Press, Dec. 6, 1993.

35. The regulations required that organizations which use US funds to support family planning in the developing world inform program participants about the full range of birth control options. (See McKeegan, pp. 85–86.)

36. Christian Action Council press release, Aug. 2, 1990.

37. *Boston Globe*, June 3, 1993.

38. *Boston Globe*, Jan. 21, 1992.

39. Catholic League publications and letter of Aug. 19, 1993 from President Donohue to Senator Joseph A. Biden.

40. On the legal conflicts and leadership succession issues see the League's 1992 audited financial statements, and articles in *Church and State* Oct. 1991, the *Wanderer* (June 17, 1993), the *National Catholic Register*, Dec. 26, 1993.

41. According to CUL's Form 990, which shows no dues–paying membership.

42. CUL's IRS Form 990s, 1990 through 1992.

43. National Charities Information Bureau, *Wise Giving Guide*: A summary of evaluations of national not–for profit organizations based on the NCIB's basic standards in philanthropy, Dec. 1993. Other financial issues also may deserve additional scrutiny. For example Joseph L. Conn ("Unholy Matrimony," *Church and State*, Apr. 1993) reports that CCA spent $50,000 on a TV political advertising campaign in 1992, but CCA's 1992 tax return contains no provision for such an expenditure.

44 "Peace on Earth, because mommy let it begin with me." (Undated CUL Christmas card soliciting financial contributions, mailed in fall 1993.)

45 CUL Form 990s, 1990 through 1992.

46 CUL Form 990 and publications list.

47 According to Fr. Paul Marx, writing in *Human Life International Reports*, No. 63, 1990.

48 Drogin, 1983 (Note that this pamphlet was still part of the basic information packet CUL mailed in response to public inquiries as of fall 1993.)

49 Drogin, 1983.

50 See the following Womanity pamphlets: *Secondary Virginity: A New Beginning; On the Verge of Virginity and Dating: A Guide for Guys 'n' Gals.*

51 *Washington Times*, Mar. 13, 1991.

52 Rice, 1985.

53 Free Speech Advocates Newsletter June 1992 and Aug. 1993; Wanderer Feb. 4, Apr. 1 and Apr. 15, 1993. On ACLJ, see also United Press International Nov. 19, 1993.

54 *Wanderer*, Feb. 13, 1992.

55 Pamphlet, "Catholics United for Life Youth Crusaders."

56 *1993 Catholic Almanac*, p. 575.

57 CUF's IRS Form 990, 1992.

58 National Charities Information Bureau, *Wise Giving Guide*: A summary of evaluations of national not-for-profit organizations based on the NCIB's basic standards in philanthropy, Dec. 1993.

59 Letter of May 2, 1973, quoted in *Lay Witness*, Sept. 1993.

60 Hebblethwaite, Peter, *In The Vatican*, Bethesda, MD: Adler & Adler, 1986

61 Lernoux, 1989, pp. 207–214.

62 Lernoux, Apr. 17, 1989; *San Francisco Chronicle*, Mar. 9, 1989.

63 *The Wanderer*, Feb. 27, 1992

64 *The Wanderer*, Aug. 22, 1989.

65 *The Wanderer*, Oct. 7, 1993.

66 *National Catholic Register*, Feb. 14, 1993.

67 *Christendom College Bulletin*: 1992–94, pp. 107–109.

68 Dr. Scholl's Foundation's Form 990PF, 1990.

69 Bellant 1991, p. 123.

70 *National Catholic Register*, Feb. 14, 1993.

71 *Bulletin*, p. 97.

72 Bellant, 1991, p. 26, on Carroll's CIA past; see Christendom literature on the school's origins and Carroll's conversion.

73 *Bulletin*, pp. v, 2.

74 *Bulletin*, p. 3.

75 *Bulletin*, pp. 21–24.

76 *Christendom College Bulletin* 1992–1994, p.14.

77 *Bulletin*, pp. 63–4, 72–3.

78 Bellant 1991, pp. 25–26.

79 *US News and World Report*, May 30, 1988.

80 Ann Gasper, *Planned Parenthood: The Professional Killers*, Washington: Concerned Women for America, Aug. 1989.

81 Grants figures for 1990–92 from Domino's Foundation Form 990PF. For earlier years see also *Detroit Free Press*, Oct. 1, 1989 and Bellant, "Domino's 'pizza tiger' linked to Word of God, *National Catholic Reporter*, Nov. 18, 1988.

82 *Detroit Free Press*, June 4, 1989.

83 See Domino's Foundation's Form 990PF, 1990–92.

84 Russ Bellant, "Domino's 'pizza tiger' linked to Word of God," *National Catholic Reporter*, Nov. 18, 1988. See also see also *Detroit Free Press*, June 4 and Oct. 1, 1989. On USAID funding for Domino's Foundation activities, see the organization's 1992 Form 990PF, which lists receipts of $250,000 from USAID. (Report of funding in the Reagan years comes from Monaghan, as quoted by Bellant.)

85 Bellant, Nov. 18, 1988, op. cit.

86 Lernoux, Apr. 17, 1989.

87 *Boston Globe* Apr. 27 and Apr. 28, 1989; Prud'homme 1990.

88 FUS Fact Sheet for 1993–94 academic year.

89 FUS Catalog, p. 1.

90 Sykes, pp. 49–51.

91 Bellant, Nov. 18, 1988 and Nov. 30, 1990. On anti-abortion activism, see also:
• undated FSU Brochure, "The Way, the Truth, and the Life;"
• *Pittsburgh Press* July 17, 1989; July 8 and Nov. 17, 1990, Apr. 8, 1991;
• Cardinal John O'Connor, "A thoroughly Catholic university," *Catholic New York*, May 21, 1992;
• *The Wanderer*, Aug. 13, 1992.

92 FSU, "The Way..". p. 10 and Catalog p. 137.

93 See Bellant, *op. cit.* and *Pittsburgh Press*, Aug. 3 and Aug. 23, 1991.

94 *Columbus (Ohio) Dispatch*, July 17, 1989.

95 *Columbus Dispatch* and *Pittsburgh Press*, op. cit.

96 *Columbus Dispatch*, Nov. 9, 1990 and Bellant Nov. 30, 1990.

97 Citizens for Life, "The Ethics of Violence in Defense of Life and Why Pro-Lifers Should Refrain from Lethal Force," position statement published Oct. 1993, signed by Juli Loesch Wiley, Monica Migliorino Miller, Edmund Miller, Mike Schmiedicke, Bishop Austin Vaughan, John Cavanaugh O'Keefe, Joseph Foreman, Chris Bell, Terry Sullivan, Chet Gallagher, Bal Dino, Vicki DePalma, Elise Rose Silverberg, Christopher M. Wight, Joan Andrews Bell, Fr. John Osterhout, TOR, and Collegians Activated to Liberate Life.

98 O'Connor, *op. cit.*

99 FUS publications, see esp. "The Way..." p. 4; FSU Catalog pp. 3–5, 47.

100 On relationship with SS, see Bellant, *op. cit.* and *Pittsburgh Press*, Aug. 3 and Aug. 23, 1991. Additional information was provided to CFFC by Bellant.

101 *Pittsburgh Press*, July 12 and Aug. 15, 1990; *Washington Post*, Apr. 8, 1993.

*Endnotes, continued*

102  Planned Parenthood profile of the Lambs, undated.

103  *Pittsburgh Press*, July 12, 1990; An Apr. 8, 1993 *Washington Post* article on Martin Wishnatsky, a **Lamb** who converted from Judaism to Mormonism, provides further insight into the Lambs' tactics and attitudes.

104  Interview with Wiley in *Pittsburgh Press*, July 12, 1990; See also *New York Times* Mar. 24, 1992.

105  *Wichita Eagle*, May 3, 1992; *Pittsburgh Press* July 8, July 12 and July 13, 1990.

106  *Wichita Eagle*, May 3, 1992; *Washington Post*, Apr. 8, 1993; On Bishop Sullivan, *The Wanderer*, Mar. 12, 1992; On Houston, *Houston Post*, Aug. 18, 1992.

107  Citizens for Life, "The Ethics of Violence in Defense of Life and Why Pro-Lifers Should Refrain from Lethal Force," position statement published Oct. 1993, signed by Juli Loesch Wiley, Monica Migliorino Miller, Edmund Miller, Mike Schmiedicke, Bishop Austin Vaughan, John Cavanaugh O'Keefe, Joseph Foreman, Chris Bell, Terry Sullivan, Chet Gallagher, Bal Dino, Vicki DePalma, Elise Rose Silverberg, Christopher M. Wight, Joan Andrews Bell, Fr. John Osterhout, TOR, and Collegians Activated to Liberate Life.

108  *The Wanderer*, Dec. 30, 1993.

109  *San Francisco Chronicle*, Dec. 7, 1991.

110  *Washington Post*, Mar. 18, 1990.

111  *Detroit Free Press* June 24, 1987, Oct. 11, 1987 and Oct. 4, 1989; see also separate listing for Domino's Foundation.

112  Washington Post, Mar. 18, 1990.

113  Lernoux, April 17, 1989; see also entries for **Knights of Malta**, **Opus Dei**, and **Word of God–Sword of the Spirit**.

114  Bellant, Nov. 18, 1988.

115  Bellant, "Domino's 'pizza tiger' linked to Word of God," *National Catholic Reporter*, Nov. 18, 1988. See also *Detroit Free Press*, Oct. 11, 1987, which reports that Silvestre had resigned from his original religious order because of its supposed "Marxist tendencies," but does not identify the order in question.

116  Prud'homme 1990; Bellant Nov. 18, 1988 and Mar. 2, 1990; Inc. Feb. 1986; *Los Angeles Times* June 29, 1990; *Restaurant Business News*, Apr. 10, 1992; *Detroit Free Press*, June 20, 1991; *Washington Post*, Mar. 18, 1990.

117  *Washington Post* Mar 18, 1990 and Bellant, op. cit.

118  *Catholic News Service*, Mar. 19, 1993.

119  "Life Insight," Jan. 1994.

120  *Catholic News Service*, Jan. 12, 1994.

121  *Catholic News Service*, Dec. 16, 1993.

122  *Catholic News Service*, Jan. 12, 1994 and Jan. 14, 1993.

123  NCCL's IRS Form 990, 1992.

124  NCCL's IRS Form 990, 1992.

125  Notes to the Financial Statements of HLF and NCCL, as filed with the New York State Department of State.

126  Telephone interview, Nov. 18, 1993, New York Department of State, Commercial Recording Division.

127  Form 990s, HLF and NCCL.

128  Attachments to NCCL and HLF Form 990s, 1992.

129  Circulation figures as listed on Form 990s.

130  Notes to NCCL Financial Statements, Dec. 31, 1992 and 1991.

131  Notes to HLF Financial Statements, Dec. 31, 1992 and 1991.

132  Aug. 3, 1993 to Senator Joseph R. Biden Jr. from the NCCL, signed by Robert McFadden.

133  *National Catholic Register*, Sept. 5, 1993.

134  From PLAL's IRS Form 990s, 1990 through 1992.

135  National Charities Information Bureau, *Wise Giving Guide*: A summary of evaluations of national not–for profit organizations based on the NCIB's basic standards in philanthropy, December 1993.

136  PLAL publications.

137  *Washington Post*, Sept. 17, 1988.

138  Weigel 1989, p. 76.

139  Various PLAL publications.

140  *Chicago Tribune*, Aug. 20, 1986.

141  Goodman, Nov. 2, 1985.

142  *The Wanderer*, Aug. 10, 1989.

143  Goodman, Dec. 1, 1984.

144  United Press International, Jan. 30, 1991.

145  *USA Today*, Sept. 15, 1991; *Washington Post*, Nov. 23, 1991.

146  Diamond Sept.–Oct. 1993; Ms. Apr. 1989; *Washington Post*, Apr. 8, 1993.

147  *Wanderer*, July 16, 1992.

148  *The Wanderer*, Feb. 27, 1992.

149  *The Wanderer*, July 16, 1992; Washington Post Oct. 4, 1984.

150  Space does not allow us to offer a comprehensive overview of the complex network of organizations associated with Word of God and Sword of the Spirit; for a more complete examination of these groups, see the writings of Russ Bellant, especially the following:
• *The Coors Connection*: *How Coors Family Philanthropy Undermines Democratic Pluralism*. Boston,: South End Press, 1991, pp. 18– 23.
• "Word of God Network wants to save the world: Right–wing alliance includes curia, big business, contras and CIA," *National Catholic Reporter*, Nov. 18, 1988.
• "Domino's 'pizza tiger' linked to Word of God," *National Catholic Reporter*, Nov. 18, 1988.
• "Millionaire says poverty is exciting," *National Catholic Reporter*, March 2, 1990.
• "Ohio university linked to antiabortion activists," *National Catholic Reporter*, Nov. 30, 1990.
• "Ohio bishop may blunt Sword of the Spirit group," *National Catholic Reporter*, June 21, 1990.
Except where otherwise noted, our discussion of WG–SS is based on Bellant's writings, and additional information supplied by Bellant in a telephone interview.

151  Bellant June 21, 1990; *Pittsburgh Press*, May 5, May 7, May 12, June 27, July 21, Aug. 3, Aug. 23 1991.

152  *National Catholic Register* May 3, 1992; *Pittsburgh Press*, June 27, 1991.

153  *The First Freedom* (a newsletter of the Puebla Institute), Sept.– Dec. 1993.

154  Interview with Russ Bellant.

155  Bellant, "Secretive Puebla Institute has ties to CIA, contras, conservative bishops," *National Catholic Reporter*, Nov. 18, 1988. For more detail on Belli and the CIA, see also Cockburn 1987.

156  *Washington Post*, Apr. 30, 1990; Cockburn 1991; *Miami Herald*, Mar. 21, 1991.

157  *Miami Herald* March 21, 1991 and Dec. 23, 1993.

158  See, for example, testimony of Nina Shea before the Subcommittee on Western Hemisphere Affairs, Committee on Foreign Affairs, US House of Representatives, July 21, 1993.

159  *The First Freedom*, Sept.–Dec. 1993.

160  Thomas Case, "TFP: Catholic or Cult," *Fidelity*, May 1989, together with letters of response in subsequent issues, is the single most useful and comprehensive English–language source on this organization.

161  TFP press release, May 31, 1990.

162  Case, p. 22.

163  See, for example, "Today, France — Tomorrow, Self Managing Socialism: the World," *Johannesburg (South Africa) Star* (and newspapers in 12 other countries, May 1, 1982; "Communism and AntiCommunism on the Threshold of the Millenium's Last Decade" (published in 60 US papers, 199) according to TFP press release of May 31, 1990.

164  *The Public Eye*, Sept. 1993, p. 8; Lernoux 1989, p. 342.

165  Case, May 1989 and *Fidelity* (letters to the editor), Sept. 1989, pp. 7–10.

166  Case, pp. 24–25; Lernoux, 1989 p. 338.

167  Lernoux 1989, pp. 340–42.

168  Case, pp. 25, 28.

169  Case, pp. 25–27.

170  Case, p. 26.

171  Letters column, Fidelity, July–Aug. and Sept. 1989.

172  Lernoux 1989, p. 343.

173  Bellant 1991, p. 21.

174  *Fidelity*, Sept. 1989.

175  O'Sullivan, 1993.

176  *Wanderer*, Oct. 8, 1993 and TFP conference announcement.

177  Lernoux, p. 343.

178  *Boston Herald*, Jan. 30, 1994.

179  This profile is drawn from WAL literature and a May 14, 1993 article in the *Boston Pilot*.

180  WFF Form 990EZs, 1990–1992.

181  *Voices*, summer 1993, p. 2

182  WFF pamphlets.

183  *St. Louis Post–Dispatch*, Apr. 1, 1990.

184  *Voices*, summer 1993.

185  *Voices*, summer 1993.

# PART IV:
# ALLIES OF THE CATHOLIC RIGHT

• • • • • • • • • • • • • • • • • • • • • • • • • • • • • • • • • • • •

## AMERICAN LIFE LEAGUE INC.

*2721 Jefferson Davis Highway,*
*Suite 101B*
*Stafford, VA 22554*
*Tel: 703–659–4171*
*Fax: 703–659–2586*

*POB 1350*
*Stafford, VA 22555*

*Affiliates at same address include:*
*African American Committee*
*Athletes for Life*
*Castello Institute (research arm)*
*Protect Life in All Nations*
*(International arm)*
*Teen American Life League/VOICE*
*Campus Outreach*

*Other affiliate:*
*American Life Lobby, Inc.*
*[501(c)(4) lobbying arm of ALL]*
*POB 490,*
*Stafford, VA 22554*
*Tel: 703–659–4173*

### MEMBERSHIP, STRUCTURE, FINANCES

*Membership*
Claims 62 autonomous affiliates with 259,000 families as members (as of 1990).

*Financial data*
**American Life League (ALL)** is a tax–exempt 501(c)(3) organization.

Lobbying is done through its 501(c)(4) affiliate, the **American Life Lobby**.

Heavily dependent on $20 membership fee, ALL reported revenue of $8.2 million in 1990 for its national office alone, and claimed about 300,000 contributors.[1]

Relatively secretive about finances and fundraising, ALL declined to cooperate with 1992 Better Business Bureau inquiry.[2]

### PUBLICATIONS AND COMMUNICATIONS

*ALL About Issues* (bimonthly 48–page news magazine; ALL claims 300,000 readers.)

### POLICIES AND ACTIVITIES

Although nominally non–sectarian, ALL is substantially Catholic in its origins, leadership and orientation and employs a Maryknoll priest as Spiritual Director.[3]

In her autobiography, founder and president Judie Brown describes how her return to the Catholic faith of her birth led directly and quickly to involvement in the antichoice movement and — after an "unfortunate" experience with a priest who tolerated contraception — to a recognition that she herself had sinned through the use of artificial contraception.[4]

ALL supports an amendment to the US constitution which would ban abortion without any exception for rape or incest (Human Life Amendment).[5] ALL has been active in organizing against sex education in public schools,[6] and has also "opposed to all forms of birth control with the exception of natural family planning."[7]

ALL's leadership and endorsers are a "Who's Who" of the right wing of Catholic antichoice action: Rev. Paul Marx of **Human Life International** chairs an ALL board that also includes top leaders of **Catholics United for Life** and the **Pro–Life Action League**. ALL's "special friends" also include Phyllis Schlafly and Paul Weyrich — perhaps the two most active Catholic participants in efforts for political convergence with the fundamentalist Protestant Religious Right. ALL fundraising literature relies primarily on endorsements from prominent Catholics to establish the group's credibility. For example, an October 1993 brochure quotes four Catholic bishops, including Cardinal Edouard Gagnon (President, Pontifical Council for the Family), Bishop James C. Timlin of Scranton, Cardinal John O'Connor of New York and retired Archbishop Daniel E. Sheehan of Omaha as endorsers of the group's work.[8]

In 1990, an ALL member active in Bishop Rene Gracida's Corpus Christi, Texas diocese founded the National Federation of Officers for Life, a nationwide antichoice group for police, state troopers and federal law enforcement officers.[9]

### PEOPLE [10]

*League Officers and Leadership:*
Brown, Judie, President
Ford, James H., MD, Executive Vice–President Emeritus
Sassone, Robert L., Executive Vice–President
Norris, Murray, Executive Vice–President
Clark, Scarlett, Recording Secretary

*American Life League Inc, continued*

Mansfield, Clay, Treasurer
O'Brien, Fr. Denis, MM, Spiritual Director
Norris, Francis, Vice President, Operations
Horn, Pastor Jerry, Vice President, Public Relations
Colliton, William F., MD, Director Medical Affairs
Harrison, Marion Edwyn, General Counsel

*Other staff, board members and key supporters*
Crum, Dr. Gary E., Director, Castello Institute
Marx, Rev. Paul, Chairman of Executive Board (Also founder
        and President, Human Life International)
Scheidler, Joseph, Executive Board Member (Founder &
        Exec. Dir., Pro-Life Action League)
LaHaye, Beverly, "Special Friend" (President, Concerned
        Women for America)
Marshall, Robert G., Director, Government Information
Sadick, Mary Heim, Public Information Director, Castello
        Institute; also Associate Director, ALLobby
Schlafly, Phyllis, "Special Friend"
Weyrich, Paul M., "Special Friend" (Founder and President,
        Free Congress Foundation)
Wildmon, Rev. Donald E., "Special Friend" (American
        Family Association)
Dornan, Rep. Robert K., (R–California)

# Concerned Women for America

*Postal: P.O. Box 65453, Washington, DC 20035*
*370 L'Enfant Promenade SW, Suite 800*
*Washington, DC 20024*
*Tel: 202–488–7000 / 800–458–8797*
*Fax: 202–488–0806*

## Membership, structure, finances

### Membership and structure

**Concerned Women for America (CWA)** claimed 600,000 members in 1992.

CWA claims to have more than 1,000 Prayer/Action groups located in every state and political action groups in many metropolitan areas. Concerned Women for America "Area Representatives" coordinate "grassroots" activity in each state, monitor state legislation, and organize congressional lobbying.

### Financial data[11]

Registered as a 501(c)(3) public charity.

Financial disclosures filed with the state of New York and the federal government contain some inconsistencies and, as of late 1993, were the subject of ongoing inquiries by officials in New York's Department of State.

Reported $8.2 million in revenue and $7.3 million in expenses in 1992; $9.3 million in revenue, $9.2 million in expenses in 1991.

Functional division of 1992 gross expenditures as reported by CWA was as follows:

- Management and general expense: 11%
- Fundraising: 26%
- Program services: 63%

However, detailed breakdowns on payments to CWA's professional fundraisers — provided to New York State — suggest that professional fundraisers may have kept more than half the money they raised for CWA. Those reports contain:

- Two conflicting figures for expenditures associated with direct mail fundraising by CWA's main fundraising counsel: Killian McCabe Associates of Dallas, Texas. KMA solicitations provided $6.67 million in gross revenue, 81 percent of the total for that year. However, one set of figures indicates that $3.06 million of this amount (46 percent of the total) was absorbed by fundraising expense; the other set of figures suggests that 100 percent was spent on fundraising.
- A telephone solicitation campaign by Mark I Communications of Ft. Worth, Texas, produced $686,000 in gross revenue, yet only $14,000 (2 percent of amount raised) in net proceeds to CWA.

According to documents in its New York state file as of October, 1993, CWA failed to provide required information on its relationship with at least two other fundraising firms and faced a potential ban on further soliciting of funds in New York.

CWA's main revenue sources are direct mail (89 percent in 1992) and telephone solicitation (8 percent in 1992). Its funding has grown dramatically over past decade (its 1984 budget was $1 million).

## Publications and communication

*Family Voice* (monthly; 200,000 subscribers);
*Issues at a Glance* (monthly); and
*CWA News Digest* (monthly produced by CWA's Education & Legal Defense Foundation)

## Policies and activities

CWA was founded in 1979 to counter the activities of the National Organization for Women generally, and to oppose passage of the Equal Rights Amendment in particular.

CWA is best known for its work on "family values" issues. It has been active in opposing abortion, gay rights legislation, and federal funding for the arts and sex education programs. The group works to censor school books and curricula — especially sex education curricula — which do not promulgate values it finds acceptable. It has supported school prayer and the teaching of creationism in public schools. Its litigation section (which employs four full–time attorneys) has joined the **Catholic League for Civil and Religious Rights** in litigation defending the "right" of landlords to refuse to rent to unmarried couples. It has cooperated with **Catholics United for Life** on antichoice litigation.

However, CWA also actively pursues a right–wing foreign policy agenda. In response to appeals from Col. Oliver North — who spoke at CWA's 1985 and 1986 conventions — the group became an active supporter of the Nicaraguan contras and other right–wing movements in Central America.

Supreme Court Justice Clarence Thomas was a scheduled speaker at CWA's 1993 convention, but withdrew in the face of adverse publicity.

## People

### Key leaders

LaHaye, Beverly, President
Lyons, Barrie, Vice President for education and field development
Jenlason, James J., Vice President for finance

*Concerned Women for America, continued*

Farris, Michael P., Vice President and (formerly) Counsel;
    also on board of CWA Legal Defense Foundation, failed
    1993 candidate for Lieutenant Governor of Virginia.

*Board members include:*
Murphy, Linda, Chair
Parshall, Janet, Treasurer
Peters, Shirley, Secretary
Brack, Paulette, Vice–President
Chapman, Lee
Chastain, Jane
Johnson, Cindy
Sieleman, Maxine
Scheck, Lori
Sindorf, Kathy
Stevens, Val
Woodall, James

# ETHICS AND PUBLIC POLICY CENTER

*1015 Fifteenth Street NW, Suite 900*
*Washington, DC 20005*
*Tel: 202–682–1200*
*Fax: 202–408–0632*

## MEMBERSHIP, STRUCTURE, FINANCES

### Membership

Not a membership organization.

### Financial data [12]

Registered as a 501(c)(3) public charity.

**Ethics and Public Policy Center (EPPC)** depends primarily on foundation and corporate grants for its funding. During the Reagan–Bush years it also became a recipient of US government funding, which provided 13 percent to 14 percent of its budget in 1991 and 1992. In 1992, three of the nation's leading conservative foundations — Lynde and Harry Bradley, H. Smith Richardson and Sara Scaife — provided about half of EPPC's budget. The US government's National Endowment for Democracy was its fourth largest funding source. Because EPPC eschews direct mail and other mass market–oriented financing mechanisms, fundraising expense is very low (3 percent of expenses in 1991).

Reported revenue of $1.24 million and expenditures of $1.21 million in 1992. Functional division of expenditures as follows:

- Management and general expense:          33%
- Fundraising (professional fundraising fees):     5%
- Program services:                   62%[13]

This expenditure barely complies with the NCIB standards requirement that at least 60 percent of funds be devoted to program services. Overhead expenditures, though still falling within guidelines, appear to have grown since the 1990 retirement of founder Ernest Lefever, and salaries for senior staff have increased substantially even after adjusting for inflation. (President Weigel's salary rose from $80,000 to $107,000; Senior Fellow Eastland's from $32,000 to $92,000.)

However, questions have been raised about financial propriety because of other financial practices.

A 1990 audit revealed apparent irregularities in the disbursement of funds from an endowment set up for EPPC by conservative funder Shelby Cullom Davis, ultimately leading to a rupture of EPPC's ties to Davis.[14] The notes to EPPC's 1992 financial statements indicate that a January 29, 1993 "Independent Auditor's report "noted certain matters involving the internal control structure and its operations."[15]

EPPC is the only organization covered by this guide for which the NCIB has conducted its own investigation of compliance with the full range of NCIB fundraising and governance standards. (Our scrutiny of other organizations covers only their compliance with standard 6a, regarding utilization of funds.) That September 1992 study concluded that EPPC has failed to comply with the following standards:

- Board governance: EPPC does not meet standards calling upon organizations to (1c) maintain an attendance policy for board members; (1e) hold "in-person, face–to–face meetings, at least twice a year, evenly spaced, with a majority of voting members in attendance; (1h) promulgate "policy guidelines to avoid material conflicts of interest involving board or staff and (1j) promote "pluralism and diversity within the organization's board, staff, and constituencies."
- Financial disclosure: EPPC fails to provide members of the public "audited financial statements or, at a minimum, a comprehensive financial summary."[16]

## PUBLICATIONS AND COMMUNICATION

Periodicals include:
*EPPC Newsletter* (quarterly on EPPC activities)
*American Purpose* (10/year; commentary on foreign policy)
*The American Character* (quarterly; commentary on domestic policy)

Recent books and monographs have included:
*Religious Liberty in the Supreme Court* (1993)
*The Price of Prophecy: Orthodox Churches on Peace, Freedom and Security* (1993)
*Education and the Public Trust: The Imperative for Common Purposes* (1993)
*American Jews and the Separationist Faith: The New Debate on Religion in Public Life* (1993)
*Might and Right After the Cold War: Can Foreign Policy Be Moral?* (1993)
*No Longer Exiles: The Religious New Right in American Politics* (1993)
*1492 and All That: Political Manipulations of History* (1992) by Robert Royal
*Freedom and Its Discontents: Catholicism Confronts Modernity* (1991)
*Just War and the Gulf War* by James Turner Johnson & George Weigel (1991)

## POLICIES AND ACTIVITIES

Founded in 1976 by Ernest W. Lefever, EPPC has served as a center for criticism of liberal church activism on economic policy and foreign affairs. It has served, and continues to serve, as the ecumenical "think tank" of neo–conservative and

## Ethics and Policy Center, continued

center–right religious thought. It has shown relatively little interest in the "family values" issues which preoccupy most religious right organizers.

Especially in its early years, its role was largely reactive, with a heavy focus on exposing allegedly "leftist" tendencies in mainline Protestant leadership. Though founder Lefever's personal pre–occupation with the "radicalism" of the National Council of Churches and the World Council of Churches was heavily stressed in these early years, Catholics — many of them critical of the US Catholic Conference (USCC/NCCB) — also participated actively in EPPC's symposia and written work, as did Jews and evangelical Protestants.

During the Reagan and Bush years, EPPC gradually shifted its emphasis away from attacks against the left toward affirmative presentations of right–of–center perspectives on social issues. There was also a gradual shift toward Catholic leadership, which now predominates, at least at the senior staff level. President George Weigel, one of the more promi-nent Catholic neoconservative thinkers, has exhibited a particular zeal both for promoting a distinctively "Catholic intellectual life" while arguing that those Catholic values very precisely support capitalist economics and American–style political democracy.[17]

Weigel and Senior Fellow Terry Eastland serve on the National Committee of the **Catholic Campaign for America**. Vice President Robert Royal is Treasurer of the Washington, DC chapter of the **Catholic League for Religious and Civil Rights**. In the 1980s and 1990s, EPPC also developed programs on "Orthodox Studies" and "Evangelical Studies."[18]

Many board and staff members — among them former UN Ambassador Jeane Kirkpatrick and former Justice Department official Terry Eastland — held significant positions in the Reagan and Bush administrations.

### PEOPLE

*Management/senior staff include:*
Weigel, George, President (1989)
Royal, Robert, Vice President for research
Lefever, Ernest F., Senior Fellow (founding President, now retired or semi–retired)
Eastland, Terry, Resident Fellow
Cromartie, Michael, Research Fellow

*Outside board members*
Zumwalt, Admiral Elmo R. Jr., Chair
Freeman, Neal B.
Glendon, Prof. Mary Ann
Haberman, Joshua O.
Henry, Carl F.H.
Hill, Frederick W.
Kampelman, Max M.
Kirkpatrick, Jeane J.
Neuhaus, Rev. Richard John
Tanham, George
Wallis, W. Allen
Whitehead, John C.

# FEMINISTS FOR LIFE

*733 Fifteenth Street, NW*
*Suite 1100*
*Washington, DC 20005*

## MEMBERSHIP, STRUCTURE, FINANCES

### Membership

Claims 4,000 members.[19]

There are numerous organizations at state and local levels which call themselves Feminists for Life, including groups in St. Louis, Missouri; Milwaukee, Wisconsin; Minnetonka, Minnesota (education project); Tucson, Arizona; Glendale, California. Some of these may operate independently.[20]

### Financial data

Not yet obtained. It is known that the "Feminists for Life Education Fund" received $10,000 from the Domino's Foundation in 1990.

## PUBLICATIONS

*Sisterlife* (newsletter)

## POLICIES AND ACTIVITIES

Founded in 1972, **Feminists for Life** describes its opposition to choice on abortion as a stance which "continu[es] the prolife feminism which goes back 100 years and affirms that women should be able to make life–affirming choices." It has actively supported the Hyde Amendment and Violence Against Women Act and opposed the Freedom of Choice Act. It supports natural family planning and opposes artificial contraception.[21]

Despite the "feminist" title, this group has no visible connections with feminist organizations of any kind and, to the contrary, works closely with the anti–feminist religious right. For example, it joined the Christian Action Council, **Concerned Women for America**, **Family Research Council**, **American Life League**, **Free Congress Foundation**, **Catholic League**, the Eagle Forum and the **Pro-Life Action League**, among others, in a drive to demand that corporations end support for Planned Parenthood.[22]

It is, however, a member of the Seamless Garment Network, a mostly Catholic group of organizations which link their stance abortion with opposition to the death penalty and nuclear weaponry.[23]

## PEOPLE

*Important leaders include:*
MacNair, Rachel, President
Wiley, Julie Loesch, Cofounder (now heads Tennessee chapter)
Goltz, Pat, Cofounder
Callahan, Cathy, Cofounder

# FREE CONGRESS FOUNDATION

*717 Second Street NE*
*Washington, DC 20002*
*Tel: 202–546–3000*
*Fax: 202–543–8425*

## MEMBERSHIP, STRUCTURE, FINANCES

### Membership

Not a membership organization.

### Financial data [24]

Registered as a 501(c)(3) public charity.

Reported revenue of $5.19 million and expenses of $4.7 million in 1992. Reported functional division of 1992 expenditures was as follows:

- Management and general expense: 8%
- Fundraising: 10%
- Program services: 82%[25]

This expenditure pattern conforms to NCIB standards. President Paul Weyrich was paid $201,258 in 1992.

Robert Russell and Associates Inc. received $165,817 in compensation for fundraising services in 1992.

## PUBLICATIONS AND COMMUNICATION

FCF's primary media activity is "National Empowerment Television," a donor and advertiser–supported 24–hour cable and satellite television channel. FCF's eight hours per day of original programming (reruns fill the balance of its round-the-clock schedule) includes a daily call–in program with Paul Weyrich, a talk show produced by the American Life League, and regular programs hosted by House Minority Leader Newt Gingrich and conservative columnist Robert Novak.[26]

Following the expansion of NET in 1993, FCF discontinued its monthly "conservative leadership" newsletter, *Empowerment!* It continues to produce *The Weyrich Insider* (a newsletter signed by Weyrich), as well as books, monographs and "special reports."

The organization also offers two series of occasional papers, emphasizing issues of concern to "cultural conservatives."

The *Policy Insights* series of issues briefs has covered topics including:

- "Medical Savings Accounts ... an Alternative to the Health Care problem;"
- "Parental Notification Laws;"
- "Examining the Foundation of Infant Mortality Programs."

The *Essays* on *Our Times* series offers longer, quasi–scholarly publications on topics including:

- *Whither Abortion? Whither the Court? Reflections on Casey and on its Consequences;*
- *Can We Afford Parental Choice?*
- *Battlegrounds in the Culture War;*
- *Declaration of Independence: Justice Clarence Thomas, One Year Later.*[27]

## Policies and Activities [28]

The **Free Congress Foundation (FCF)** was founded in 1977 by Paul Weyrich, who continues to head it. Weyrich had earlier cofounded the Heritage Foundation (1973) as a tax exempt New Right research center and the politically activist Committee for survival of a Free Congress (1974). The key to each group's creation was funding from the Coors (breweries) family of Colorado, whose foundation remains a primary funding sources for both Heritage and FCF. Weyrich has devoted his career to the creation of a popular constituency for views rooted in a kind of populist nativism which often verges on racism.

Among New Right groups in Washington, FCF is noteworthy for its leaders' and officers' lack of squeamishness about connections to racist, terrorist and anti–Semitic groups which others might find repugnant or, at minimum, deeply embarrassing. Board member Charles Moser has served on the editorial advisory board of the *Ukrainian Quarterly*, a publication which has offered praise for the Waffen SS and defended World War II Ukrainian collaboration with the Nazis.[29] Kathleen Teague Rothschild served simultaneously on the boards of FCF and the US branch of the neo–fascist–linked World Anti–Communist League. Weyrich himself hired convicted Nazi collaborator Laszlo Pasztor — who was forced out of the Bush campaign when reports on his past surfaced in 1988 — to staff the FCF–based Coalitions for America.[30]

Among the conservative "think tanks," it has been FCF's distinctive role to bring far right Catholics — including those who identify with the literally reactionary **Tradition, Family and Property** or the Charismatic–authoritarian **Word of God–Sword of the Spirit** network — together with their Protestant fundamentalist counterparts. In the 1980s, FCF developed a Catholic Center — headed first by anti–gay crusader Fr. Enrique Rueda and later by Michael Schwartz — which played an important role in the development of a self–consciously Catholic wing of the Religious Right. FCF staff members Connaught and William Marshner also played a key role in these efforts, as did Weyrich himself. (See **Christendom College**, TFP and WG–SS entries.)

Reorganization in the 1990s eliminated the Catholic Center name from FCF's lists of affiliates, but Weyrich,

Schwartz and others continue its work. Schwartz, who now directs FCF's Center for Social Policy, is also chairman of the board of Life Decisions International, a group founded in 1992 to "challenge Planned Parenthood and its philosophy throughout North America and the world," and is a former official of the **Catholic League for Religious and Civil Rights**.[31]

Current major divisions of FCF are:

- **National Empowerment Television**, FCF's largest current budget item (annual budget $2.1 million). This cable and satellite network broadcasts conservative political programming 24 hours a day as "a direct challenge to the usual television establishment;"[32]
- The **Krieble Institute**, providing training for current and future leaders in the former Soviet Union and Eastern Europe;[33]
- The **Center for Conservative Governance**;
- The **Center for State Policy**;
- The **Center for Social Policy**;
- The **Center for Law & Democracy**; and
- The **Center for Cultural Conservatism**.

## PEOPLE

*Paid, full-time officers*
Weyrich, Paul, President
Dingman, Richard B., Exec. Vice Pres.
Swanson, Rosemary, Vice President
Weyrich, Diana J., Vice President for Development

*Officers of affiliated groups (Weyrich is president of each affiliate)*
Krieble Institute: Krieble, Dr. Robert H., founder
Exnicios, John, Vice President

*National Empowerment Television*
Bennett, William J., Chairman
Pines, Burton Yale, Vice–Chairman

*Selected senior staff*
Jipping, Tom
Gannon, Paul
Lind, William
Schwartz, Michael

*Unpaid officers and board members*
Coors, Jeffrey H., Chairman
Krieble, Dr. Robert H., Vice–chairman
Hall, Cong. Ralph M., Secretary
Beckett, John D., Treasurer
Anderson, T. Colman, III
Armstrong, Sen. William L.
Heinz, Clifford S.
Kohler, Terry J.
Magruder, Marion Jr.
Moser, Dr. Charles A.
Roe, Thomas A.
Rothschild, Kathleen Teague
Sandblom, Robert L.
Smith, Henry J.

# INSTITUTE ON RELIGION AND PUBLIC LIFE

*156 Fifth Avenue, Suite 400*
*New York, NY 10010*
*Tel: 212–627–2288*
*Fax: 212–627–2184*

MEMBERSHIP, STRUCTURE, FINANCES
*Membership*
Not a membership organization.

*Finances*
Details were not obtained in time for inclusion in this report.

PUBLICATIONS AND COMMUNICATION
*First Things* (monthly)

POLICIES AND ACTIVITIES
The **Institute on Religion and Public Life** is a neoconservative–oriented center for "interreligious, nonpartisan research and education" designed to "advance a religiously informed public philosophy for the ordering of public life." It is similar in orientation to **Ethics and Public Policy Center**, with which it has significant overlap of leadership, authors and seminar participants.

Its most visible activity is publication of *First Things*, a monthly magazine which serves as a forum for semi–scholarly articles promoting conservative views on sexuality, gender, race relations, and family structure. The magazine's writers also periodically attack what they view as dangerously left–wing trends in both Protestant and Catholic religious thinking and church social action. The Institute sponsors scholarly conferences, consultations, research projects, public education events, and a fellows program. The Institute is headed by Richard John Neuhaus, a former Lutheran pastor who became a Catholic priest in September 1991.[34]

Neuhaus, who previously headed a New York branch of the "paleoconservative" Rockford Institute, created his current organization in 1989 following a dispute which became the symbol of divisions between nativist, often–isolationist, "paleoconservatives," and the east coast– dominated "neoconservative" movement.

After Neuhaus criticized Rockford Institute President Allan Carlson for publishing articles which "belittle[d] the gravity of anti–Semitism as a moral evil," Rockford Institute staff members came to New York to physically evict Neuhaus from his office. Soon thereafter, at a Rockford Institute–sponsored conference, self–proclaimed "paleoconservative"

Lew Rockwell defined 'paleos' as those who "are opposed to the post–FDR belief in mass democracy — which they see as leading to the welfare state — and ... reject internationalist crusades to spread global democracy." Rockwell — and many others after him — have identified Patrick Buchanan as the most important spokesman for this faction of the right.[35]

In the context of a guide to the Catholic right, it is certainly worth noting that both Buchanan and another likely presidential contender from the "neoconservative" camp, William Bennett, are Catholics who stress the connection between their political views and their religious values.

PEOPLE
*Board, management and senior staff include*
Neuhaus, Rev. Richard J., President and Editor–in–Chief of *First Things*
Novak, David, Vice–President
Weigel, George, Secretary–Treasurer
Berger, Peter, Senior Advisor
Nuechterlein, James, Associate Director; Editor of *First Things*
Goldman, Davida, Assistant Director
Berke, Matthew, Managing Editor, *First Things*
Decter, Midge, Distinguished Fellow
Dalin, David, Senior Fellow
Hutcheson, Richard G. Jr., Senior Fellow
Vaughan, Richard A., Publications Director

*Institute council members include*
Berger, Brigitte, Boston University
Burtchaell, James, Congregation of Holy Cross
Derr, Thomas, Smith College
Elshtain, Jean Bethke, Vanderbilt University
Fortin, Ernest, Boston College
Garment, Suzanne, American Enterprise Institute
Glendon, Mary Ann, Harvard Law School
Hafen, Bruce, Brigham Young Law School
Hauerwas, Stanley, Duke Divinity School
Loury, Glenn, Boston University
Novak, David, University of Virginia
Weigel, George, Ethics and Public Policy Center

ENDNOTES

1  Financial data and leadership information is drawn primarily from a 1991 profile of ALL, prepared by Planned Parenthood; it has <u>not</u> been updated for this report.

2  Telephone interview with BBB's Philanthropic Advisory Service.

3  *All About Issues*, Nov.–Dec. 1993.

4  Judie Brown, *It is I who have chosen you: An Autobiography*, Stafford, Virginia: ALL, 1992.

5  ALL Pamphlets: "Dealing with Exceptions" and "Rape and Incest Exceptions to Abortion Law: Why they are bad policy."

6  *Washington Times*, June 13, 1989.

7  Judie Brown, quoted in Goodman 1985.

8  Organizational literature supplied by ALL.

9  *The Wanderer*, Dec. 17, 1992.

10  League officers and leadership as listed in *All About Issues* Nov.– Dec., 1993; listings of other significant figures drawn from an Oct., 1993 fundraising mailing, other ALL literature and press reports.

11  Sources: CWA's New York State Annual Financial Report (Charitable Organization) for its fiscal years ending June 30, 1992 and June 30, 1991; Form 990 for fiscal year ending June 30, 1991; CWA Contract for direct mail services with Killion McCabe & Associates, June 10, 1992; Resource Development Inc, "Agreement to Provide Services for Concerned Women for America," March 1992; Steve Cram & Associates, "State of New York Statement(s) attached to and made part of professional fundraiser registration," July 14 and Nov. 13, 1992; Contract between Mark I Communications Inc. and Concerned Women for America, Jan. 29, 1990.

12  EPPC's 1992 Form 990, New York State disclosure filings and audited financial statements; National Charities Information Bureau, "Ethics and Public Policy Center." (Report # 544, Sept. 18, 1992.)

13  CCA's IRS Form 990, 1992.

14  George Weigel, Memo to the Executive Committee re: Shelby Cullom Davis Investment Fund, May 3, 1991. (As filed with the New York State Secretary of State.)

15  The full text of the report is a public document submitted to the National Endowment for Democracy and the US Information Agency. It has not been examined, however, in the preparation of this study.

16  National Charities Information Bureau, "Ethics and Public Policy Center." (Report #544, Sept. 18, 1992.)

17  See Weigel, 1989 and *National Catholic Register*, May 17, 1992.

18  Sources for entry include EPPC newsletters (1993); *Washington Post,* Oct. 4, 1993; Coulson 1987; Weigel 1989; Griffith 1981.

19  Scheinin, 1993.

20  1991–92 Pro–Life Directory.

21  *National Catholic Register*, July 18, 1993.

22  Christian Action Council Press Release, Aug. 2, 1990.

23  Scheinin, 1993.

24  FCF Form 990, 1992.

25  CCA's IRS Form 990, 1992.

26  *Washington Times*, Dec. 6, 1993.

27  "Free Congress Foundation Publications Listing, Spring 1993" and update supplied by FCF.

28  In the space available here, it is not possible to provide a comprehensive portrait of one of the New Right's most important institutions. For further information see Bellant 1991, pp. 1–35.

29  Bellant 1991, p. 31.

30  Bellant 1991, p. 28–32.

31  Life Decisions International, "Who are We: Oh No! Not Another Pro–Life Group!," The Caleb Report, Jan–Feb. 1993, V. 1, No. 1.

32  FCF mailing, November 1993.

33  Form 990, 1992.

34  *New World* (Chicago Archdiocesan newspaper), Sept. 13, 1991.

35  Diamond, 1990. For a "paleoconservative" perspective on the split, see Gottfried, 1993.

# SELECTED REFERENCES

• • • • • • • • • • • • • • • • • • • • • • • • • • • • • • • • • • • • • • • •

REFERENCE BOOKS, LEGAL DOCUMENTS AND
RESEARCH REPORTS

Aldridge, Dawn, ed. *1991–92 Pro–Life Resource Directory*.
Los Angeles, CA and Glasgow, Scotland: International
Life Services, Inc., 1990.

Clarkson, Frederick & Porteous, Skipp. *Challenging the
Christian Right: The Activist's Handbook*. Great
Barrington, MA: Institute for First Amendment Studies,
Inc., 1993.

*Catholic Almanac* 1993. Edited by Foy, Felician A. OFM,
Huntington, Indiana: Our Sunday Visitor, 1993.

National Charities Information Bureau, *Wise Giving Guide*: A
summary of evaluations of national not–for–profit organizations based on the NCIB's basic standards in
philanthropy, Dec. 1993.

New York State, Office of Charities Registration, *The
Solicitation and Collection of Funds for Charitable Purposes*
(Article 7–A of the Executive Law).

_____. Annual Financial Report — Charitable
Organizations. (As submitted by various organizations
listed in the guide.)

*Official Catholic Directory 1993*. P.J. Kenedy & Sons, 1993.

People for the American Way. Profiles of individual groups,
Feb. 1993.

Planned Parenthood Federation. Profiles of individual
groups, 1992.

United States Internal Revenue Service, *Cumulative List of
Organizations described in section 170(C) of the Internal
Revenue of 1986*, Revised to Sept. 30, 1992.

_____. Return of Organization Exempt from Income
Tax, Form 990 (as filed by various listed organizations).

Various publications of listed groups.

*Who's Who in America* (online edition, electronically searched
via Compuserve).

PERIODICALS AND WIRE SERVICES

*Adweek's Marketing Week*
*Boston Globe*
*Business Month*
*Christian Century*
*Chicago Tribune*
*Church and State*
*Columbus Dispatch*
*Cult Observer*

*Detroit Free Press*
*Free Speech Advocates*
*Journal of the American Medical Association*
*Jornal de Brasilia*
*Los Angeles Herald–Examiner*
*Milwaukee Journal*
*Ms.*
*The Nation*
National Catholic News Service
*National Catholic Reporter*
*National Catholic Register*
*New York Post*
*New York Times*
*Pittsburgh Press*
PR Newswire
*Restaurant Business News*
*San Francisco Chronicle*
*St. Louis Post–Dispatch*
*US News and World Report*
United Press International
*USA Today*
*The Wanderer*
*Washington Post*
*Washington Times*
*Washington Watch* (monthly newsletter of the Family Research
Council)
*Wichita Eagle*
*Who's Who*

FINANCIAL DATA SOURCES

Better Business Bureau (BBB)
National Charities Information Bureau (NCIB)
New York Department of State, Office of Charities
Registration
US Internal Revenue Service (IRS)

BOOKS AND ARTICLES

Allen, Charlotte, "What They Preach . . . ; . . . and What They
Practice: Lifestyles of the Right and Famous," *Washington
Post* (Outlook Section), October 17, 1993.

Anderson, Scott and Jon Lee Anderson, *Inside the League: The
Shocking Exposé of How Terrorists, Nazis and Latin
American Death Squads Have Infiltrated the World Anti–
Communist League*. New York: Dodd, Meade &
Company, 1986.

## Selected References, *continued*

Ball, William Bentley, "*Why Can't We Work TOGETHER?* A noted Catholic lawyer urges Catholics and evangelicals to become partners in the battle against rampant secularism," *Christianity Today*, July 16, 1990.

Barnes, Fred, "The Baby face–off," *The New Republic*, May 9, 1988.

Bellant, Russ. *The Coors Connection: How Coors Family Philanthropy Undermines Democratic Pluralism.* Boston, MA: South End Press, 1991.

_____, "Word of God Network wants to save the world: Right–wing alliance includes curia, big business, contras and CIA," *National Catholic Reporter*, Nov. 18, 1988.

_____, "Domino's 'pizza tiger' linked to Word of God," *National Catholic Reporter*, Nov. 18, 1988.

_____, "Millionaire says poverty is exciting," *National Catholic Reporter*, Mar. 2, 1990.

_____, "Ohio university linked to antiabortion activists," *National Catholic Reporter*, Nov. 30, 1990.

_____, "Ohio bishop may blunt Sword of the Spirit group," *National Catholic Reporter*, June 21, 1990.

Benestad, J. Brian, *The Pursuit of a Just Social Order: Policy Statements of the U.S. Catholic Bishops, 1966–80.*

Berlet, Chip, "Cardinal Mindszenty: heroic anti–Communist or anti–Semite or both?," *St. Louis Journalism Review*, Apr. 1988.

Bozell, L. Brent III, "Statement of L. Brent Bozell III, Chairman, Media Research Center, on media coverage of papal visit," Catholic Campaign for America, Aug. 25, 1993.

Brown, Judie. *It is I who have chosen you: An Autobiography.* Stafford, VA: ALL, 1992.

Case, Thomas, "TFP: Catholic or Cult," *Fidelity*, May 1989. (And letters of response published in the July–Aug. and Sept. issues of the magazine.)

Catholics For a Free Choice. *The Bishops Lobby.* Washington, DC, 1991.

Christendom College. *Bulletin 1992–1994.*

Citizens for Life, "The Ethics of Violence in Defense of Life and Why Pro-Lifers Should Refrain from Lethal Force," position statement published Oct. 1993, signed by Juli Loesch Wiley, Monica Migliorino Miller, Edmund Miller, Mike Schmiedicke, Bishop Austin Vaughan, John Cavanaugh O'Keefe, Joseph Foreman, Chris Bell, Terry Sullivan, Chet Gallagher, Bal Dino, Vicki DePalma, Elise Rose Silverberg, Christopher M. Wight, Joan Andrews Bell, Fr. John Osterhout, TOR, and Collegians Activated to Liberate Life.

Cockburn, Alexander, "Vicious and wrong," *The Nation*, June 13, 1987.

_____. "The P.C. crusade in Nicaragua," *The Nation*, June 10, 1991.

Coleman, John A., "Who are the Catholic Fundamentalists," *Commonweal*, Jan. 27, 1989.

Conason, Joe, "The Religious right's quiet revival," *The Nation*, Apr. 27, 1992.

Conn, Joseph L., "Unholy Matrimony," *Church and State*, Apr. 1993, pp. 4–6.

Costello, Gerald M. *Without Fear or Favor: George Higgins on the Record.* Mystic, Connecticut: Twenty Third Publications, 1984.

Coulson, Chester, "A taste for pork: defunding the right. (federal aid to conservative groups)," *New Republic*, Mar. 2, 1987.

Crilly, Scholastica, O.S.B., "A critical look at 'the Work,'" *National Catholic Register*, May 2, 1993.

Diamond, Sara. *Spiritual Warfare: The Politics of the Christian Right.* Boston, MA: South End Press, 1989.

_____, "No place to hide," *The Humanist*, Sept.–Oct. 1993.

_____, "Rumble on the right," *Z Magazine*, December 1990.

Drogin, Mrs. Elasah, "Obedience: The Key to a Catholic Pro–Life Victory," (CUL pamphlet, 1983).

Fanlo, Leandro, "Blessed Josemaria Escrivá: sanctity for the laity," *Living City* (Focolare Movement magazine), Nov. 1992.

Farrell, Michael J., "What Escrivá's beatification says about church," *National Catholic Reporter*, Apr. 17, 1992.

Feuerherd, Joe, "Bishop hobnobs with cardinals to woo church," *National Catholic Reporter*, Dec. 29, 1989.

Franciscan University of Steubenville, *1993–94 Catalog: Be Bold, Be Catholic, Be Educated.*

_____, *The Way, the Truth, and the Life.* (Undated promotional brochure, distributed to potential students as of Nov. 1993.)

Gasper, Ann. *Planned Parenthood: The Professional Killers.* Washington: Concerned Women for America, Aug. 1989.

Goodman, Ellen, "Terrorists — Here at Home," *Washington Post*, Dec. 1, 1984.

_____, "Voodoo Biology," *Washington Post*, Nov. 2, 1985.

Gottfried, Paul E., "Conservative Crack–Up Continued," *Society*, Jan.–Feb. 1994.

Griffith, Carol Friedley ed. *Christianity and Politics: Catholic and Protestant Perspectives.* Washington: Ethics and Public Policy Center, 1981.

Hawkinson, Kandace, "A life of piety, and a life of pain," *Milwaukee Journal*, Mar. 31, 1984.

Hebblethwaite, Peter. *In The Vatican.* Bethesda, Maryland: Adler & Adler, 1986.

Higgins, Msgr. George G. *Organized Labor and the Church.* New York: Paulist Press, 1992.

Kahn, Gabriel, "League takes new tack," *National Catholic Register*, Dec. 26, 1993.

Kamm, Henry, "The Secret World of Opus Dei," *New York Times Magazine*, Jan. 3, 1984.

Lee, Martin, A, "Who are the Knights of Malta," *National Catholic Reporter*, Oct. 14, 1983.

_____ and Kevin Coogan, "The shady chivalry of the Knights of Malta," May 23, 1986.

Lernoux, Penny, "The papal spiderweb – I: Opus Dei and the 'perfect society,'" *The Nation*, Apr. 10, 1989.

_____, "The papal spiderweb - II: a reverence for fundamentalism," *The Nation*, Apr. 17, 1989.

_____, "Who's Who? Knights of Malta know," *National Catholic Reporter*, May 5, 1989.

_____, *People of God: The Struggle for World Catholicism*, New York: Viking Penguin, 1989.

Luker, Kristin. *Abortion & the Politics of Motherhood*. Berkeley, CA: University of California Press, 1984.

Mahony, Archbishop Roger, "Statement of the Archdiocese on Operation Rescue," *The Tidings*, Aug. 11, 1989.

McCarthy, Colman, "The Right Hand of The Church," *Washington Post Book World*, Nov. 8, 1992.

McKeegan, Michelle. *Abortion Politics: Mutiny in the Ranks of the Right*. New York: The Free Press, 1992.

National Conference of Catholic Bishops and United States Catholic Conference, *Agenda Report Documentation for General Meeting – Action Items 1–10*, Washington, DC Nov. 15–18, 1993.

_____, *Agenda Report Documentation for General Meeting – Information Items*, Washington, DC Nov. 15–18, 1993.

Neuhaus, Richard John, "Speaking for the Public Good," *First Things*, Nov. 1993.

Neuman, Elena, "A holy terror from the right?" *Insight*, Jan 11, 1993.

Occhiogrosso, Peter. *Once a Catholic*. Ballantine Books, 1987.

O'Connor, Cardinal John, "A thoroughly Catholic university," *Catholic New York*, May 21, 1992.

Oliveira, Plinio Correa de. "Today, France — Tomorrow, Self Managing Socialism: the World," *Johannesburg Star*, May 1, 1982.

Opus Dei Awareness Network, "Educational Packet," 1993. (A collection of articles, pamphlets and other materials on Opus Dei.)

O'Sullivan, Gerry, "Catholicism's New Cold War: The Church Militant Lurches Rightward," *The Humanist*, Sept.–Oct. 1993, pp. 27–32.

Prud'homme, Alex, "Is there life after pizza? (The Profile: Tom Monaghan)" *Business Month*, Mar., 1990.

Reardon, David, The Seduction of Feminism, CRNET (electronically published) 1992.

The Resource Center (Albuquerque), "GroupWatch" reports on Americares, Concerned Women for America and Opus Dei.

Rice, Charles E., "Abortuary Bombing — the Justification Defense, and Sidewalk Counseling," *The Wanderer*, June 27, 1985.

Roche, Dr. John J., "Winning Recruits in Opus Dei, A Personal Experience," *The Clergy Review*, Oct. 1985.

_____, "The Inner World of Opus Dei," typed manuscript, Sept. 7, 1982.

Scheidler, Joseph M. *Closed: 99 Ways to Stop Abortion*. Tan Publishers.

Schmitt, WIlliam A., "Opus Dei Responds to Odan," *Crossroads* (the newsletter of the Catholic Campus Ministry Association), Oct. 1992.

Shaw, Russell, "The Secret of Opus Dei," *Columbia*, 1982.

Shell, Adam, "Controversies over social issues causing firms to re-examine policies: growing activism, greater press scrutiny pose new internal and external dilemmas," *Public Relations Journal*, June 1990.

Stan, Adelle-Marie, "Like a prayer," *New Republic*, July 6, 1992.

Sykes, Charles and Miner, Brad, eds. *The National Review College Guide: America's 50 Top Liberal Arts Schools*. New York: Wolgemuth & Hyatt, 1991.

Tribe, Lawrence. *Abortion: The Clash of Absolutes*. New York: W.W. Norton, 1990.

Walsh, Michael. *Opus Dei: An Investigation into the Secret Society Struggling for Power within the Roman Catholic Church*. New York: HarperCollins, 1992.

Weigel, George. *Catholicism and the Renewal of American Democracy*. Mahwah, New Jersey: Paulist Press, 1989.

Wheaton, Kathleen, "The men who could be king (of Brazil)," *Town & Country Monthly*, Apr. 1993.

Young South Africans for a Christian Civilization, "The Municipal Elections and Apartheid," *The Citizen*, Johannesburg, Oct. 22, 1988 (full page advertisement)

_____, "TFP: Fighting Communism on All Levels," *The Windhoek Advertiser*," Nov. 21, 1988.

# APPENDIX

## CATHOLICS FOR A FREE CHOICE

*1436 U Street, NW, # 301*
*Washington, DC 20009*
*Phone 202–986–6093*
*Fax 202–332–7995*

### MEMBERSHIP, STRUCTURE, FINANCES

*Membership*
Not a membership organization.

*Affiliates*
Católicas por el Derecho a Decidir, Montevideo, Uruguay (Latin American regional affiliate)
Católicas pelo Direito a Decidir, São Paulo, Brazil
Católicas por el Derecho a Decidir, Mexico City, Mexico

*US network*
Catholics for a Free Choice (CFFC) reports approximately 100 activists in 40 states and territories and Canada. These activists organize and speak publicly to further CFFC's educational goals in their local communities. Some of these activists have set up local organizations. While CFFC does not operate or finance the local groups, CFFC provides technical assistance, materials, and guidance. Local organizations exist in California, New York, Massachusetts, Ohio, Wisconsin, Colorado, Hawaii, Kansas, Minnesota, Missouri, Montana, Oregon, Rhode Island, Texas, Washington, and West Virginia.

*Financial data [1]*
Registered as a 501(c)(3) public charity.
Reported revenue of $1.27 million and expenditures of $1.14 million in 1992. Functional division of 1992 expenditures was as follows:

- Management and general expense: 3%
- Fundraising: 7%
- Program services: 90%

This expenditure conforms to NCIB standards, which state that organizations should "spend at least 60% of annual expenses for program activities."[2] Revenue has grown annually at least since 1987, when it was $366 thousand. Most of CFFC's funds come from foundation sources, and the organization makes no significant attempts at fundraising through direct mail.

### PUBLICATIONS AND COMMUNICATION

*Conscience* (quarterly English–language newsletter of prochoice Catholic opinion)
*Consciencia* (quarterly Spanish–language newsletter on reproductive health issues in Latin America, produced by Católicas por el Derecho a Decidir")
*Instantes* (quarterly newsletter of CFFC's Latina Initiative)

*Pamphlets*
- "Abortion: A Guide to Making Ethical Choices" (also in Spanish)
- "Bishops on Birth Control: A Chronicle of Obstruction"
- "Contraception in Catholic Doctrine: The Evolution of an Earthly Code" (also in Spanish)
- "Guide for Prochoice Catholics: The Church, the State and Abortion Politics"
- "History of Abortion in the Catholic Church" (also in Spanish, Portuguese, and Polish)
- "Public Perceptions: The Bishops Lobby"
- "Reflections of a Catholic Theologian on Visiting an Abortion Clinic"

### POLICIES AND ACTIVITIES

Three New York women who had been active in the National Organization for Women — Joan Harriman, Patricia Fogarty McQuillan and Meta Mulcahy — formally launched CFFC in 1973. In the early years, the group had neither office, staff, nor budget, and leaders worked out of their homes.

In the early 1970s, the group focused primarily on defending the right to take a prochoice stance within the church, and challenging the doctrinal basis for the church's ban on abor-

*Catholics for a Free Choice, continued*

tion. In one early manifestation of this orientation, Jesuit Fr. Joe O'Rourke, a then–active priest who was on the CFFC board, challenged then–Boston Cardinal Humberto Madeiros' edict banning Catholic baptism for a baby born to a prochoice mother. O'Rourke baptized the baby on the steps of a church. (The Jesuits dismissed O'Rourke on account of this incident.) Later in the decade, CFFC became increasingly involved in prochoice political action. After Pat McMahon became executive director in 1982, CFFC's emphasis shifted from lobbying to education, and the organization developed a growing connection with movement among Catholic feminists for a women–centered church.[3]

Frances Kissling succeeded McMahon as executive director in 1982. Though Kissling has tried to take a "less reactive" approach to the bishops, stressing "abortion as a moral issue, rather than a subject of church legalisms or secular law," her tenure has been marked by deepening confrontation with the church hierarchy as it grew increasingly militant in its opposition to abortion. An October 1984 "Catholic Statement on Pluralism and Abortion," sponsored by CFFC, asserted that "a diversity of opinions regarding abortion exists among committed Catholics." The ad became the touchstone for this new confrontation. The cautiously–worded statement took no stand on the morality of abortion, merely arguing that dissent on the subject had a legitimate place inside the church. Nonetheless, the Vatican forced priests and nuns who signed to choose between repudiating the statement or suffering expulsion from their canonical communities.[4]

CFFC's Latin American branch, Católicas por el Derecho a Decidir, grew out of a 1987 meeting with Latin American Catholic women in Costa Rica. The branch is based in Uruguay with national affiliates in Brazil, Nicaragua, and Chile. CFFC has also supported projects in Mexico, Poland and Ireland.

CFFC's Latina Initiative was launched in 1992 to provide information on reproductive health care and public policy to Hispanic and Latina organizations in the United States.[5]

Since the late 1980s, CFFC has increasingly sought dialogue with those who have moral qualms about abortion and stressed the need to provide the services which make abortion unnecessary. The new approach was suggested by Kissling in a 1988 speech. "The arguments, the circumstances, that won legal abortion and legal contraception in this country are different today," she said. "The majority of the people in this country ... are both prochoice and conservative about abortion. They are not comfortable, totally comfortable, with how they believe the right to abortion has been exercised." It is epitomized by a 1992 CFFC advertisement reads as follows:

"NOBODY WANTS TO HAVE AN ABORTION
"Picture a world where mothers have easy access to childcare they can afford. Where children can count on a good education no matter what school district they live in.

Where people have healthcare whether or not they have a job. Where safe birth control is available to everyone who needs it. In this world, abortion isn't illegal. It's unheard of. Isn't that the best choice of all?"[6]

*On sexuality and reproductive issues* [7]
"**Church teaching on sexual and reproductive issues is not infallible**. Moreover, the church has no teaching on when the fetus becomes a person."

"**Abortion** can be a moral choice. Women can be trusted to make decisions that support the well–being of their children, families, and society, and that enhance their own integrity and health."

**Abortion law**: "A Catholic who believes abortion is immoral in all or most circumstances can still support its legality."

**Contraception**: "[C]ontrary to the conventional wisdom, the morality of artificial contraception is by no means a closed subject within the Catholic church. It is a matter of continuing and lively discussion within the hierarchy, among theologians and by lay Catholics."

**Lesbian and gay rights**: "[M]any Catholic theologians have supported the principle that both heterosexual and homosexual domestic partnerships based on justice and commitment, rather than the traditional marital contract, are morally valid."[8]

**Reproductive health funding**: "Poor women are entitled to non–discriminatory public funding for childbearing and for their reproductive health, including abortion and family planning."

**On the fetus** (personal statement by Kissling): "I value the fetus because it is human, that is, of our species, living, and as such represents all our hope for the future of humankind... I feel that the value of the fetus, until the third trimester, never outweighs the value of women's well–being or the social importance of acknowledging women's capacity to weigh all the values in making the decision whether or not to continue a pregnancy... I believe that as the fetus comes closer to fulfilling its potential to become a person, more serious reasons are required to morally justify terminating its life. I do not believe that my beliefs in this realm are more factually compelling than [others'], and thus I am unwilling to see any one of our beliefs enacted into law." [9]

*On other issues*
**Church authority**: "Church law affirms both the right and the responsibility of a Catholic to follow his or her conscience, even when it conflicts with church teaching."

**Women's ordination**: Women's opportunities to serve the church in key policy positions are severely limited by the legacy of prior canonical norms, by clericalism, by sexism, and by the continuing unwillingness to open fully all ministries, including ordination, to women."[10]

**Economic justice**: "The Catholic social justice tradition calls us to stand with the poor and other disadvantaged groups."

## PEOPLE

*Leadership and key staff*
Kissling, Frances, President
Lebel, Greg, Public Affairs Director
Lombardi, Karen, International Program Director
Shannon, Denise, Education and Communications Director

*Board of directors*
Hennessey, Patricia, Chair
Collins, Stephen, Treasurer
Hunt, Mary, Secretary
Bonavoglia, Angela
Gordon, Mary
Maguire, Daniel C.
Marcos, Sylvia
Milhaven, Giles
Moran, Eileen
O'Rourke, Joseph
Valencia–Greene, Lori
von Vacano, Marcela
Wilderotter, Peter

Católicas por el Derecho a Decidir
Grela, Cristina, Coordinator

## ENDNOTES

1. From IRS Form 990s, 1991 and 1992.
2. National Charities Information Bureau, *Wise Giving Guide*: A summary of evaluations of national not–for profit organizations based on the NCIB's basic standards in philanthropy, Dec. 1993.
3. Shannon 1993, pp. 53–54.
4. Hunt and Kissling, 1987.
5. *Instantes*, April 1993.
6. *Conscience*, Spring/Summer 1993.
7. Position statements taken from undated pamphlet, "Catholics for a Free Choice," unless otherwise noted.
8. CFFC press release, Sept. 17, 1993.
9. *Conscience*, Spring 1992.
10. CFFC press release, Nov. 12, 1988.

# INDEX

● ● ● ● ● ● ● ● ● ● ● ● ● ● ● ● ● ● ● ● ● ● ● ● ● ● ● ● ● ● ● ● ● ● ● ● ●

## A Catalogue of Individuals Mentioned in this Directory

*An individual's organization is listed only when the person has an official tie to a group listed in this directory. Where the individual has no such affiliation to an organization listed in this directory, page numbers only are used.*

*A Catalogue of Individuals Mentioned in this Directory, continued*

*A Catalogue of Individuals Mentioned in this Directory, continued*

*A Catalogue of Individuals Mentioned in this Directory, continued*